Welcome EVERYTHIN

D0373204

These handy, accessible books give you all you need to tackle a difficult project, gain a new hobby, comprehend a fascinating topic, prepare for an exam, or even brush up on something you learned back in school but have since forgotten.

You can read this EVERYTHING® book from cover to cover or just pick out the information you want from the four useful boxes: Card Questions, Shark Bites, Johnny Quads' Corner, and Texas Truths. We literally give you everything you need to know on the subject but throw in a lot of fun stuff along the way, too.

We now have well over 300 EVERYTHING® books in print, spanning such wide-ranging topics as weddings, pregnancy, wine, learning guitar, one-pot cooking, managing people, and so much more. When you're done reading them all, you can finally say you know EVERYTHING®!

? *Card Questions*
Common Hold'em questions answered.

Shark Bites
Quotes from the pros.

Johnny Quads' Corner
Tips from Johnny Quads himself.

Texas Truths
Hold'em history and facts.

THE

EVERYTHING.
Series

Dear Reader,

Texas Hold'em barged into my life while I was playing for nickels in the 1960s. That was back when poker was cool, before it got uncool and now is cool again.

It wasn't called Hold'em then. The neighborhood Huck Finn who introduced the variation to our group of grade schoolers called it Hold Me Darling, and when he turned those first three community cards face-up, all hell broke loose. Being Stud and Draw players, we were shocked at this madness.

Every time it was Huck's deal, he'd try again, but the game didn't catch on with us kids. We favored games where you could play a ton of hands, with lots of action. Hold'em, however, is a serious player's game where patience, betting skill, playing premium hands, and reading opponents gets you the money.

In time, I graduated to higher-stakes home games and Vegas, but by the '80s poker didn't get my blood rushing like it used to. But one fateful day at a casino, as my boring Stud game broke up, a middle-aged card cutie whispered in my ear, "Why don't you try Hold'em?" I did, somehow I won, and in an explosion of clarity I saw the deceptive simplicity, the beauty, and the deep complexity of this amazing game. I've never looked back.

Since then, Hold'em's been my game and I have never had a losing year. Follow this book closely and you will have the same success and, like Huck Finn rafting down the Mississippi, will be off on the adventure of a lifetime.

Johnny Quads

www.johnnyquads.com

THE
EVERYTHING®
TEXAS HOLD'EM BOOK

Tips and tricks you need
to take the pot

John "Johnny Quads" Wenzel

Adams Media
Avon, Massachusetts

An Everything® Series Book.
Everything® and everything.com® are registered trademarks of
F+W Publications, Inc.

Published by Adams Media, an F+W Publications Company
57 Littlefield Street, Avon, MA 02322 U.S.A.
www.adamsmedia.com

ISBN 10: 1-59337-579-4
ISBN 13: 978-1-59337-579-9

Printed in Canada.

J I H G F E D C

Library of Congress Cataloging-in-Publication Data
Wenzel, John.
The everything Texas hold'em book : tips and tricks you need to take
the pot / John 'Johnny Quads' Wenzel.
p. cm. -- (An everything series book)
ISBN 1-59337-579-4
1. Poker. 2. Poker--Rules. 3. Gambling systems.   I. Title. II. Series:
Everything series.
GV1251.W46 2006
795.412--dc22

2005029892

This publication is designed to provide accurate and authoritative information
with regard to the subject matter covered. It is sold with the understanding that
the publisher is not engaged in rendering legal, accounting, or other professional
advice. If legal advice or other expert assistance is required, the services of a com-
petent professional person should be sought.

    —From a *Declaration of Principles* jointly adopted by a Committee of the
American Bar Association and a Committee of Publishers and Associations

Many of the designations used by manufacturers and sellers to distinguish their
products are claimed as trademarks. Where those designations appear in this
book and Adams Media was aware of a trademark claim, the designations have
been printed with initial capital letters.

This book is available at quantity discounts for bulk purchases.
For information, please call 1-800-289-0963.

THE
EVERYTHING
Series

EDITORIAL

Publishing Director: Gary M. Krebs

Associate Managing Editor: Laura M. Daly

Associate Copy Chief: Brett Palana-Shanahan

Acquisitions Editor: Gina Chaimanis

Development Editor: Rachel Engelson

Associate Production Editor: Casey Ebert

PRODUCTION

Director of Manufacturing: Susan Beale

Associate Director of Production: Michelle Roy Kelly

Cover Design: Paul Beatrice,

Erick DaCosta and Matt LeBlanc

Design and Layout: Colleen Cunningham,

Holly Curtis, Sorae Lee

Series Cover Artist: Barry Littmann

To my mother, who knows bridge, who knows writing, but who doesn't have a clue about poker.

• • •

Contents

Top Ten Texas Told'em: Quotable Quotes

A♥ "I don't lose because I have nothing to lose. Including my life." —Doc Holiday, *Gunfight at the OK Corral*

2♥ "To lose patience is to lose the battle." —Mahatma Gandhi

3♥ "In the thick of the evening when the dealing got rough, She was too pat to open and too cool to bluff." —Grateful Dead, *Scarlet Begonias*

4♥ "You call this one and it's all over, baby!" —Scotty Nguyen before winning the World Series of Poker

5♥ "Be happy with the world. Be delighted. For there are other games, always another game. There are honest men. And we, my friend . . . we are still alive." —the late Nick the Greek

6♥ "Chance favors the prepared mind." —Louis Pasteur

7♥ "My wife made me join a Bridge club. I jump off next Tuesday." —Rodney Dangerfield

8♥ "Many the Wednesday evening, escaping from a domestic or professional crisis, I settled at the table as if my noisy buddies would protect me from life itself. . . ." —author John Updike

9♥ "Life is like a game of poker. You have to take chances to win." —John "Red" Morrison

10♥ "Virtually all the greats have gone broke at least once in their careers, and I'm no different. The key is to learn something from the experience." —poker champ Daniel Negreanu

Introduction

You've heard the name, bouncing around somewhere in the recesses of your mind. Texas Hold'em. It's some card game, you think, maybe poker. The kids are playing it after school, college students are dealing it in their dorms and frat houses, and now your neighbor's even talking about playing it with his beer buddies. The moms are talking about having "girls' poker nights." Folks at work are competing online every day for real money against players from all over the world.

On TV, card sharks are winning millions of dollars, and every night there's a new show: *The World Poker Tour*, *The World Series of Poker*, *Celebrity Poker Showdown* with those movie stars, and more. Ben Affleck won $350,000 playing this crazy-looking game. The bestselling Christmas gift last year was a Hold'em table and chips!

So you wonder, What the heck is it?

In short, it is the face of modern poker, and poker has taken the country by storm. Hold'em is a game that is startling in its simplicity but filled with a lifetime of subtlety and complexity.

And these nuances could cost you, and cost you dearly—if you don't know what you're doing—because poker is all about money. It can't be played without it.

A big reason Hold'em has become so popular is that top players love it, and they love it because they think they can make more money with less risk than with other games. But you don't have to be a pro to enjoy it. Anyone can learn the rules in a few minutes and try his or her luck. And while you will never get to race against Dale Earnhardt Jr. or try to guard Lebron James—and if you did, you would have no chance—amateur players take on the most skilled poker pros in the world all the time, and sometimes come out victorious.

Part of Hold'em's beauty is that all skill levels can enjoy it. You get two cards and make a decision. The game works whether it's played for high stakes or around the kitchen table. For "action" players who like to play a lot of hands, the game is very fast, with many more hands per hour than with traditional poker, and there are times when a loose style of play can bring home the bacon. On the other hand, tight players who can patiently wait for premium hands can win big money at high-stakes Hold'em, where there is less chance of an inferior hand running them down than with other variations.

Hold'em's five community cards link your hand forever to those of your opponents. So, when that river (final) card hits the board, will it make you rich, or drown you? Will the dealer make your dreams come true, or sell you down the river? Dash your hopes with the turn of a card, or make you rich and a household name?

Either way, you will know you're alive, with your nerves vibrating, your eyes opening wide, and your heart thumping like a big bass drum. That's living. That's poker, baby!

Chapter 1
Hot, Hot, Hot!

That's poker. It's on everyone's lips these days, no longer just the domain of those backroom denizens and risk-takers living on the edge. The opportunities for viewing and playing are so abundant that instead of struggling to find a game, today's players must set limits or they'd be playing around the clock. Some folks argue that Texas Hold'em has exploded because poker has once again captured the national spirit, but that's backward. The reason poker is popular is the unique nature of Hold'em itself.

A Place to Begin

This comprehensive book on Hold'em is a starting point. Reading can help, but it is no substitute for experience, and sometimes that experience can be expensive. Realize that there is no recipe for playing every hand, and no magic formula to transform you from novice to pro, or everyone would be an expert. You need to get out there and play, and then objectively analyze your play later. Every hand. Learn and remember, but be careful, because poker can be counterintuitive.

Don't Learn Your Lesson

If you ever stuck your finger in a light socket as a child and got the shock of your life, you never did it again. You learned your lesson. But some of your worst losses in poker happen when you have great cards and have played correctly. These shocking defeats are hard to forget. You bet big with pocket kings, and an ace flops and someone beats you with aces. Does that mean you shouldn't bet strongly with kings, the second-best starting hand in all of Hold'em? Of course not. There was only an 18 percent chance of that ace hitting the flop and matching your foe's ace. And if you include all five shared cards, he won't even hit his ace a third of the time.

The same goes for the times you fold trash hands like 9-3 offsuit (different suits). What if the flop comes 3-3-9? Does that mean you should've played that loser because you would've gotten a full house? Heck, no. That miracle flop won't happen again in a thousand hands. You were absolutely correct to dump it. Playing that hand would cost you in the long run. So don't bat an eye, even though if it happened to the rookie next to you, he'd be slapping his forehead and throwing a fit.

Card Questions

What is a "bad beat"?
If you had a pot sewn up and some long-shot river card hits the board to take it away from you, that's a bad beat. Like if your heavy-favorite pocket aces lose to pocket deuces when a deuce comes up on the final card. You were a 21-to-1 favorite but still lost.

Say you're in a tournament and someone calls your all-in bet with pocket fives. You have pocket aces. You are dealt aces once every 221 hands. It's the best starting hand and you're a 4-to-1 favorite, which is about as good as it gets in Hold'em. You must bet the farm with that holding, even though the fives will dent your wallet once every five hands.

Anything can happen on a given hand in poker. That's what makes it interesting, and that's what gives poor players hope. But if your aces are "cracked" (meaning they were beaten even though you had pocket aces) and you lose, unlike the kid with his finger in the electrical outlet, you must make the same aggressive play again next time. When you are the favorite to win, you bet big to maximize your profits, and if that means betting every penny, then so be it. That's poker. Make the underdogs, or the chasers, pay to try to beat you. If they want to fold and give you the "pot" (all the money that's been bet), that's fine too.

Don't turn timid just because someone ran you down a few times and you lost a bundle. Over the long term, your proper play will make big money, even though you might be rudely shocked occasionally.

Think Long Term

In poker, you must always take the long view. Making correct decisions based on the odds and your knowledge of the game and your opponents will make you a winner. Not on every hand, not even in every game, perhaps not even every month, but over time, you will win. Winning means fun. And winning means money.

Always keep in mind that each poker hand is just a small skirmish in a larger battle, which is the game you are playing in on a particular day. But more important, that daily battle is part of a larger entity, the war. The war is your total poker-playing life, all the hands in all the games from now until you reach that big casino in the sky. The war is significant—that's where you need to come out ahead. You will win some skirmishes, lose some, and avoid a lot of them. If you use solid strategies like those in this book, and especially if you play against less-skilled foes, you will win more battles than you lose. At the end of the night, you will be a winner more often than not. And that will lead to victory in your personal poker war.

Here's Some Free Advice

Be aware that some poker pros who've written books freely admit that they keep more than their cards close to their vests. For example, near the end of *Getting the Best of*

It, prolific poker-theory author David Sklansky writes: "You may have noticed I included nothing about Lowball Draw. This is because at this writing, it is the main game at which I make my living. Which leads me to one last comment: Pros don't go around teaching others the really important things for nothing just to show how smart they are."

Take the so-called advanced books out now. The Hold'em version tells you exactly which hands to play in every position relative to the dealer. It turns out that the book's strategies are pretty much right-on for a $300- to $600-limit game popular in a famous Strip casino. Of course, the authors don't tell you that, or they wouldn't sell so many volumes. But every local in Vegas fancying himself or herself a pro (or new Internet wannabe) buys this weighty tome and uses its tactics when playing in low-limit no-fold'em fests like $4–$8 and $6–$12, which are very different games requiring different strategies, as you will learn later.

 ### Shark Bites

"Never criticize another man's way of playing his hand . . . A man who buys his chips is entitled to play them any way he wants to."
—WSOP champ Amarillo Slim Preston

And woe to the poor guy who plays some hand not on the list and beats a local out of a pot! He will definitely hear about how he won with a hand that he "never should've played" (even when it turns out upon reflection that in that particular game, the hand might have been perfectly correct to pursue). By the time the book players are through berating him, he'll wish he'd never won the hand.

Or take high-profile pro Phil Hellmuth Jr.'s popular book *Play Poker Like the Pros*. Hellmuth has umpteen World Series of Poker (WSOP) bracelets and has won millions on the tournament circuit. He is considered a master at reading players and figuring out what cards they are holding. That is his claim to fame. But in the 400 pages of his book, do you think there is a chapter on reading players? Nope.

So, keep in mind that some authors write solely for some extra cash, not so you can sit down and take food out of the mouths of their friends.

Is Tight Right?

Until now, most books have encouraged play that is too conservative and cautious. This is called "tight" in poker circles, and players who are tight to a fault are disdainfully known as "rocks." Now, don't get the wrong idea. Cautious is a good way to start. You don't want to lose all your money playing questionable cards before you have learned the game. But you can't stay tight. Tight is predictable, and being predictable is what top players want you to be. It's easier to take your money that way.

You have to understand when and how to loosen up, especially in the low- and middle-limit games that you start out playing. Except where no-limit is mentioned (mostly in the tournament chapters), the strategies in this book are tailored to low-limit and middle-limit Hold'em.

Texas Truths

There are four words that are used frequently when describing playing styles: **loose**, playing a lot of hands; **tight**, playing very few hands; **passive**, betting and raising rarely; and **aggressive**, betting and raising frequently.

A Winding Road

The journey from playing a little tight, which is the best way to start out, to knowing when and how to loosen up is a long and arduous one. Frankly, most players never complete the journey. They stay lost in the wilderness of quiet play. You'll see them all over Vegas playing low-limit games based on some book they read twenty years earlier, sitting on their leather butts waiting for the nuts.

Card Questions

What is the "nuts"?
The "nuts" is the best-possible hand with any given board in Hold'em. For example, if the board is 2-2-J-9-6, the best possible hand is four deuces—two deuces on the board and two deuces for hole cards. If there are three spades onboard and no pair, the best-possible hand, or the nuts, is an ace-high flush.

Paying Your Dues

There used to be a home game where new guys were told when they first sat down: "New players never win here." This wasn't arrogance or meanness. It was a way of softening the blow, because regulars didn't want "one-game wonders"—people who sat down, lost, and never came back.

They were trying to say: "You need to know the players to win, and you are at a big disadvantage being a stranger. It is easier for seven people to learn how one new guy plays than for one new guy to learn how seven strangers play. Just knowing cards is not enough." That's common sense. There is a learning curve in poker. Everyone has paid his or her dues. Keep that in mind if you sit down with a bunch of locals who all know each other.

Hold Me Darling

Today's poker evolved from the Draw poker games of the 1800s to the Five-Stud and Seven-Stud games so popular during World War II to, finally, an obscure game called Hold Me Darling that came out of Texas in the 1960s. It wasn't long before the Texas drawl changed the moniker to Hold'em, and the action nature of the game ensured its growth. The community cards meant that more than eight players could play, and risk-loving players embraced it because they could see a lot of cards (with lots of company). The road gamblers loved it because they knew it was much more complicated than it seemed, and most people played much looser than they should have.

Texan Felton McCorkindale brought the new game to the Golden Nugget in downtown Vegas in 1964, which at the time was only spreading lowball draw, Seven-Stud, and six-card lowball Stud (six-card Razz). Hold'em quickly took over. While it would be a decade before it made an impact on the Strip and started to catch on elsewhere, by the time Benny Binion perfected the poker tournament with the first World Series in the early '70s, Hold'em was the pros' game, the big dog. No-limit Hold'em, the Cadillac of poker, was the professionals' game of choice to decide the best in the world, as it is to this day. Not surprisingly, the first eight world champions were from Texas.

 Shark Bites

"Hold'em was a new game that offered the best platform for developing multiple strategies and tactically implementing them."
—Texas road gambler Crandell Addington

Keep the Fun in It

Remember as your career evolves that Hold'em is a game. It is an amazing game, and it is supposed to be stimulating and fun. If it ceases to be enjoyable, you have to ask yourself why you are playing. Of course, it is more fun to win than to lose, and anyone who actually enjoys losing should certainly consider getting some help. Yes, in a friendly low-stakes game, you can enjoy yourself win or lose, but everyone knows it is more fun to win. As they say: "Everything's funny when you've got the money." In fact, for most people, winning and fun are directly related. Who enjoys giving money away? Nobody! And no one wants to be the table loser night after night. The fact that you bought this book means you feel the same, because this book is all about how to win on the green felt.

Whether you approach the game as a science, an art, or as psychological warfare, your object is to win and win as much as you can. Even the world's best players endure losing streaks, but if losing breaks your spirit or your finances, you're playing over your head and it is no longer a game. The same logic applies if your victories bring no joy. So, win and have fun, but keep it in perspective because there are more important things in this world.

 Johnny Quads' Corner

If you consider not calling a bet because you are concentrating on what the money you are risking will buy, you are playing too high. Risking any money not earmarked for recreation—such as rent or food money—is a big mistake. Using that money will hurt your game and your life.

The Poker Democracy

Poker can be anything you want it to be: high-stakes hand-to-hand combat, a vacation diversion at the casino, fast-paced action online from the comfort of home or at work while the boss isn't looking, tournament play against the best players in the world (or the local $25 buy-in crowd), or a friendly, rowdy game with lots of beer and your buddies. A precious few even try to make a living at it. It's all good.

Poker is the great equalizer. There is no class system at the tables. Anyone with a buy-in can sit down and take a shot. There are no social barriers, and often you will be competing in a game with people from cultures you would never encounter in your daily life. It's not unusual in a California cardroom to find yourself facing Japanese, Mexicans, Hawaiians, Koreans, Chinese, whites, and blacks of both sexes and multiple generations *all in the same game*! Some opponents you will swear hail from another planet. It's great! And yes, even though poker was a "man's game" back in the days of the smoke-filled rooms, women are more than welcome today.

In tournaments, there is no seeding and no privilege. You pay your money, and you are treated the same as the most seasoned, famous pros. You can go to another country, sit down at a table, and play a perfectly good game without even knowing the language.

 ## Texas Truths

The four modern suits, which evolved in fifteenth-century France, had serious meanings. Spades signified the state, hearts the church, diamonds represented merchants, and clubs were the farmers. The kings were modeled after famous people: spades, David (Israel); hearts, Alexander the Great (Macedonia); diamonds, Julius Caesar (Rome); and clubs, Charlemagne (Holy Roman Empire). The joker was invented in America.

The Twenty-First-Century Poker Boom

Congratulations are in order: You couldn't have picked a better time to enter the green-felt fray. Today, poker is hot! But it wasn't always that way.

In the 1990s, poker was fading. Boys weren't brought up playing the game as they had been in earlier generations. Fathers weren't teaching it to their kids who had their noses buried in video games. In the early days of political correctness, poker was considered gambling, and gambling was not a good thing.

 Johnny Quads' Corner

> The first World Series of Poker in 1970 had a field of only seven players, but it was the toughest field ever. They were the seven best players in the world.

On average, players were getting older and older, and the game's image as something engaged in by shady characters in back rooms didn't help. Poker rooms in Vegas were becoming an endangered species. Longtime rooms at Harrah's, the Golden Nugget, Caesars, Stratosphere, Las Vegas Club, 4 Queens, Tropicana, the Flamingo, and many others closed. No one wanted to play with a bunch of ornery old men trying to grind out a few bucks, and that's pretty much what was in the casinos.

Then, just in time, some amazing things happened to salvage this beautiful game. First, a quality movie about the game hit the big screen in 1997. *Rounders*, starring Matt

Damon and Edward Norton, really grabbed you by the throat (and had some pretty good poker tips in it, too).

Second, the World Poker Tour (WPT) hit the airwaves on the Travel Channel, and the show was great. The two-hour dramas allowed the viewer to be a fly on the wall for all the final-table action at major tournaments. You even saw the hole cards!

Third, online poker took off. Novices could now learn at home, instead of having to stare down serious players.

Then, unbelievably, in 2003, the aptly named Chris Moneymaker beat 838 of the best players in the world to win the Big One—and he had never competed in a real tournament before! The only games he had played in were online, where he won his entry in a $39 satellite! This was huge. His well-publicized victory gave hope to all players piddling with their mice on the Internet.

All this media coverage—movies, TV, and the Internet—has fueled today's craze. The WSOP only attracted a few hundred entries in the 1990s and fewer than a hundred in the early '80s, but thanks to online satellites—indeed, satellites everywhere—the event has reached circus proportions.

 Texas Truths

The World Series of Poker's $2.5 million first prize in 2003 was the richest prize ever in a sport until 2004, when amateur Greg Raymer won $5 million. In 2005, Joe Hachem broke the record again by winning an incredible $7.5 million.

Tournaments are reporting record entries, and this new interest is boosting poker in brick-and-mortar casinos, college campuses, and homes around the world. Vegas casinos can't add tables fast enough, when just a few short years ago they were yanking them out to make way for slot machines. Today, an estimated 50 million to 80 million Americans play the game regularly.

Welcome to a brave new world!

Chapter 2
First Things First

You have to learn to walk before you can run. You have to win a dollar before you can win a thousand. You have to win a small diamond-horseshoe ring before you can win a World Series of Poker bracelet. And you must know the rules and protocol before you can learn the tricks and tactics. This chapter will give new players the basics of poker in general and Hold'em in particular, and I'll explain why expert players love this game.

Square One

Before we tackle the rules, here's a brief primer on the basics. Hold'em uses a standard fifty-two-card deck (no jokers). There are thirteen different cards (called ranks); the ace is the highest card, followed by the king, queen, jack, ten, nine, eight, seven, six, five, four, three, and two.

There are four suits: spades and clubs are black, and hearts and diamonds are red. Color and suit have no value in poker. A five-high straight flush in diamonds has the same value as a five-high straight flush in clubs. If both these holdings occur during the same hand, it is a tie and the pot is split. In seven-card games like Hold'em, you do not use the sixth and/or seventh cards to break ties. A poker hand consists of your best five cards only. The other cards are not used.

Jacks, queens, and kings—the deck's royalty—are called face cards or "paints."

 Texas Truths

Queens are often called ladies, kings are nicknamed cowboys, aces are bullets, jacks are hooks (from "fish-hooks"), sevens are walking sticks, eights are snowmen, threes are treys, and twos are universally called deuces or "ducks." The king of hearts is the "suicide king," and the king of diamonds is "the man with the axe."

Each hand of poker is its own game, and during an evening, you might play more than a hundred hands. You will not play each hand all the way to its conclusion, of course. More often than not, you will fold (quit the hand) early. You win a hand if all other players fold or if you have the best (highest) hand at the "showdown," which is after all the cards have been dealt and the final bets have been made and called (matched). If you win, you take all the money wagered during that hand. The harder a hand is to obtain, the more valuable it is.

The rank of the hands from best to worst follows.

Royal Flush

The royal flush is the holy grail of poker, and it is so rare that you may never hold one in your hands. It is a combination of the highest straight (A-K-Q-J-10) and the highest flush—five cards of the same suit. Only four of these combinations exist out of some 2.5 million possible five-card hands.

Straight Flush

Straight flushes are the same as royal flushes—five cards in a row of the same suit—except they are not headed by an ace. Straight flushes are also rare; the odds of getting one in five cards are 72,192 to 1. Straight flushes range from K-Q-J-10-9 to 5-4-3-2-A. A king-high straight flush, of course, beats a five-high.

Four of a Kind

This hand is made up of four cards of identical rank, as in 9-9-9-9-K. This is also a monster hand. With four of a kind, you hold every card of that rank that exists in the deck. Naturally, the higher the rank is, the higher the hand is. Note that the fifth card, called a "kicker," is irrelevant to the value of this hand.

Full House

A full house, often called a "full boat" or "boat," is three cards of one rank and two of another, as in 7-7-7-2-2 or K-K-K-9-9. The value of the full house is determined by the rank of the three of a kind, so the "kings full of nines" version mentioned here beats the "sevens full" hand.

Flush

A flush is five cards of the same suit (e.g., five clubs or five diamonds) that are not in a row. The value of the flush is determined by its high card. A flush with an ace will beat a flush headed by a king, and a Q-9-8-7-5 flush beats a Q-9-8-7-4 flush.

 Johnny Quads' Corner

The ace is the highest card, so it can make the highest straight (A-K-Q-J-10). But it also can function as a "one" in a low straight or low straight flush, as in 5-4-3-2-A. A five-high straight is known as a "wheel." A five-high straight flush is a "steel wheel."

Straight

A straight is five cards in a row of differing suits, such as Q-J-10-9-8 or A-K-Q-J-10. The high card decides the value of a straight, so 6-5-4-3-2 beats 5-4-3-2-A.

Three of a Kind

This hand holds three cards of the same rank, as in 9-9-9-4-2 or K-K-K-6-5. The higher the "trips," the better the hand; the other two cards are irrelevant.

Two Pair

This hand consists of two pairs and a fifth unrelated card, which is used only in the very rare event of a tie. The high pair determines the value of the hand, so A-A-2-2-5 beats K-K-Q-Q-J.

One Pair

This hand is one pair and three unrelated cards, which are used only to break ties, so J-J-9-8-5 beats J-J-9-8-4. Otherwise, a pair of aces beats any other pair; a pair of kings beats queens, and so on.

No Pair

A "no pair" hand, also known as a "high card" hand because the highest card determines the hand's value, is basically nothing. In a "high card" hand, you hold none of the previously described hands. If you were playing five-card Draw poker, half your hands would be nothing, and in Hold'em, half the boards will be this hand—just five unrelated cards. At the showdown, the high card wins, all the way down to the last card in case of ties. So, A-6-5-4-2 beats K-Q-J-10-6 and 10-9-8-7-4 beats 10-9-8-7-3.

The following chart shows the odds against being dealt different hands in five cards. You can equate this with the first five cards you get in Hold'em (hole cards plus the flop). This is also what you can expect to see on the board (the five community cards).

Odds Against Holding Poker Hands in Five Cards

Hand	Odds
Royal Flush	649740 to 1
Straight Flush	72192 to 1
Four of a Kind	4164 to 1
Full House	693 to 1
Flush	508 to 1
Straight	254 to 1
Three of a Kind	46 to 1
Two Pair	20 to 1
One Pair	1.37 to 1
No Pair	1 to 1

Note: The odds above are the odds against seeing these hands in five cards. So, you will see two pair on the board, for example, just once out of twenty-one hands.

The Rules of Texas Hold'em

Hold'em is a seven-card game with two hole cards and five community (shared) cards. Out of those seven, players make their best five-card hand; the high hand wins. Hold'em uses a blind system of forced bets described later in this chapter. After the blinds have put in their bets, each player is dealt two cards face-down, followed by a round of betting. After the first betting round, three community cards are placed face-up in the center of the table, called the "flop." After a round of betting a fourth card is placed face-up, called the "turn," followed by another betting round. Then the final shared card, called the "river," is placed, followed by the final round and the showdown. (The turn is sometimes called "fourth street," and the river is often referred to as "fifth street.")

To make her hand, a player may use both her hole cards and three from the board, one hole card and four from the board, or play all five cards on the board.

Play always proceeds to the left (clockwise). In the first betting round, the player to the left of the big blind acts first. In all other rounds, the player to the left of the dealer must act first. At the showdown, the cards speak, regardless of the players' declarations. For example, if a player says he has three of a kind but in fact has a full house and someone points that out or he belatedly realizes his error, he gets credit for the full house (as long as the cards have not been tossed into the muck pile). A player cannot miscall a hand. Similarly, if a player says she has a full house when she really has trips, then she has trips. Only the cards matter.

The last player to bet or raise—in other words, the player who has been "called"—shows his cards first, followed by the rest of the players proceeding to the left.

 Johnny Quads' Corner

If all other players fold, you win the pot no matter what cards you hold. You do not have to show your cards, even if someone asks to see them. They haven't paid for the privilege of seeing your hand, so don't show it. Don't give away information!

Betting Limits

Most Hold'em games use a two-tiered, fixed-limit betting structure. In a $5–$10 limit game, for example, the maximum bet during the first two rounds is $5; in the final two rounds, it is $10. Those are the only two bets allowed; there is nothing in between. Often, there is a cap on the number of raises, usually three or four. So if you are in a $10 round with a three-raise limit, the most you could put at risk is $40.

No-Limit

In no-limit Hold'em, of course, you can bet all your chips at any time, or just a few, with some stipulations. First, you can never bet or raise less than the big blind. Second, you can never raise less than the previous bet. For example, the big blind is $10 and a player raises $100. It is now $110 to you to call the bet. If you wish to raise, you must raise at least $100. If you decide to raise $100, you place $210 in the pot. You can go "all-in" (betting all of your chips) at any time, regardless of the amount.

Pot-Limit

Pot-limit is only slightly less scary than no-limit. In pot-limit, you can bet up to the amount of the pot at any time but never less than the big blind or previous bet. One nuance to watch out for is that your "call" is considered part of the pot. Say there is a $50 pot, and someone raises the "pot." This means he has made a $50 bet, which makes the pot $100. To call, you put in $50, but if you want to raise the pot, you have to raise not $100, but $150! This is because your call is considered part of the pot. So to raise the pot, you would toss in $200.

Table Stakes

No matter the limit, in all casino games and most home games, "table stakes" are played, meaning you can never put at risk more cash and chips than you have on the table. A player cannot go digging into his pocket for cash during play. If a player runs out of chips or cash during a hand, she puts the last of her chips in the pot and announces, "All-in," at which point the other players will begin to build a "side pot" with the amount the all-in player was not able to call, as well as all future bets. The all-in player is not eligible to win the side pot.

If the hand is "heads-up" (only two players), the player with more chips matches what the all-in player has put in the pot. Then the hand is played out with the cards turned face-up and with no more betting.

Card Questions

What is the "button"?
The button is the white plastic disk that cardrooms use to determine which player is the "dealer," since the deal isn't passed as it is in a home game. After every hand, the button moves one player to the left. The player to the left of the button is dealt first and always acts first.

The Blind Structure

Hold'em and Omaha, its close cousin, do not use the traditional poker ante system in which each player puts money into the pot before the deal. Hold'em uses blinds; these are forced bets that two players must place in front of themselves before the hand begins to give people something to fight for. Without blinds or antes, a player could conceivably sit and wait for the nuts all night and not be penalized for it.

Small Blind, Big Blind

The small blind is the player to the left of the dealer. She places half the minimum bet in front of her. The player to her left is the big blind. He places one full minimum bet in front of him. If you are playing in a $4–$8 game, in which the minimum bet is $4 and the maximum is $8, the small blind is $2 and the big blind is $4. Being to the left of the dealer, with the deal (and all betting action) always going to the left, the blinds are dealt first. After the first round, if they are still in the hand, the blinds will be the first to act.

Johnny Quads' Corner

Not understanding the blinds is a dead giveaway that you are a new player. Make sure you know what's going on and place your blind bet without having to be prompted by the dealer.

After everyone has received two down-cards, the "under the gun" player (the person to the left of the big blind) must match the big blind's forced bet, raise, or fold. Other players have the same options. When action reaches the small blind, she can raise (if the maximum number of raises has not been exhausted), call, or fold. The half bet she has already made counts toward what she owes.

For example, if she has $2 in the pot and someone has raised the $4 big blind to $8, the small blind owes $6 to stay in the hand. She may also raise by putting in $10, making the total bet $12 "to go." If no one has raised the big blind, the small blind may complete her bet by adding $2 to the $2 already in the pot, thus matching the big blind's $4.

The big blind may also raise in the same fashion as the small blind. The only difference in this example of a $4–$8 limit game is that he starts with $4 already in the pot, while the small blind has only invested $2. Don't think of the blinds as a penalty or as money thrown away, think of them as what they are: bets you have made that others must either call or quit the hand.

 ### *Texas Truths*

Blinds are "live"; that means that you can raise even if other players have not raised your blind bet. If you are the big blind, and the other players who have not folded have only called your $4, you still can raise by adding another $4 to make it $8. Small blinds can raise as well.

The Option

If you are the big blind and no one has raised the blind bet that you placed in the pot prior to the deal, the dealer will say, "Option" to you, which means you have a choice of raising or just calling. To raise, put in an amount equal to your blind bet. If you do not wish to raise, rap the table or say, "Check." Because your blind bet is in the pot, you can stay in the hand without putting in another penny. Knowing and acting quickly on the option is a sign of an experienced player. Not understanding the option and acting clueless or sitting there with a blank look pegs you as a rookie.

Once someone has raised your blind, you no longer have the option of checking. You must call, raise, or fold.

Blinds are not a good place to be in Hold'em. You will be forced to act first during all betting rounds except the first, and putting in money before you have looked at your cards is never desirable! Plus, smart players know you have to bet without knowing your cards, so they will be raising to make you fold and forfeit those blind bets.

For the most part, the only time both blinds and antes are used in Hold'em is in the late stages of major poker tournaments, when the limits are high.

 Texas Truths

If you miss your blinds by being away from the table, you will have to post them when you return. Posted blinds are treated the same as any blind—they are a bet. You will act on your option the same as if you were the big blind, and you have the option of checking or raising.

When the Action's on You

The money you win in Hold'em comes from winning pots, and pots are built by bets. You bet to maximize your profit on a particular hand or to press a perceived advantage. When it's your turn to act, you can check, bet, or fold. If you check, you opt not to bet, but you are still in the hand. If you fold, you quit the hand, but you should never fold unless someone else has bet. Betting is how you get more money in the pot, and you should bet if you feel your hand is the favorite to win.

If someone else bets before you, you no longer have the option of checking. You must call, fold, or raise. Folding saves you the expense of calling the bet. Calling matches your foe's wager and keeps you in the hand, as long as no one else raises. Raising is the strongest action; you've hit the ball back into the bettor's court.

It is always a good idea to say, "Raise" when you are raising, so there is no mistake. If you haven't verbalized your intention, you can run into a problem with "string bets." These bets, in which a player puts her chips into the pot in dribs and drabs, are not allowed in poker. Your money must go into the pot all at once if you are raising, unless you first say that you are raising and how much.

How Many Chips Should I Buy?

Never buy in for the minimum in a casino Hold'em game. You want enough chips to play an aggressive game and withstand any early losses. Buy in for at least $100 in chips in a $4–$8 game, $200 in $6–$12, $300 in $8–$16, and $500 in $10–$20. (If you're in a $2 game at the Palm Beach

Kennel Club, $60 should do you.) Buy enough chips so you are not the short stack at the table. You should also have enough cash for a second buy-in. If you don't, you are competing at too high a limit.

If your stack gets short, buy some more chips. You do not want to be out of ammo when you finally get a great hand.

 Shark Bites

There's an old gambling saying: "The guy who invented poker was smart, but the guy who invented chips was a genius."

Poker Table Protocol

There are some very definite dos and don'ts that keep a poker game running smoothly and amicably. These rules of etiquette include acting in turn, not "splashing" the pot (put your bets in front of you), being ready to act when the action's on you, keeping your cards in sight (on or above the table), not showing your cards to others (whether in the hand or not), and keeping out of disputes that do not involve you. Playing "partners" with another player or playing against a particular player in a different manner is resented. Talking about your cards is also frowned upon, whether you are telling the truth or lying. Not following procedure and etiquette slows or disrupts the game and pegs you as a novice.

Texas Truths

> If you win cash during a hand or sell chips to someone during a game, you must keep those greenbacks on the table. Also, do not keep chips in the plastic racks during play; it slows the game.

Don't discuss the hand, whether you're involved in it or not, and when you fold, keep the identities of your cards to yourself. Don't discuss others' strategies. If you win a pot, just rake in the chips; don't rub it in or do a postmortem on the hand. Don't abuse the other players or the dealer in any way.

Also, don't "call" the board. If three of one suit flop, don't shout out, "Who's got the flush?" If there's 9-8-7-6-5 on board, don't point out that there's a straight out there. By mentioning it, you are helping others play the hand, thereby breaking the "one player to a hand" rule. In poker, it's best to shut up during play. Save your talk for between hands.

Johnny Quads' Corner

> If you have won a hand, do not release your cards from your hands until the dealer passes you the pot.

Most of all don't be a downer. If you're losing or suffer a bad beat, don't make everyone around you miserable by acting as though it's life or death. And don't criticize the way others play their hands, no matter how angry you are or how poorly you think they play. Giving "lessons" at the table is boorish, and it's ludicrous to do it when you're losing.

Why the Pros Love Hold'em

Expert players don't like surprises. They make their loot by figuring out what other players are holding and then acting on that information. With only two hole cards, the unknowns are fewer in Hold'em than in a game like Seven-Stud, with its three hole cards, or Omaha, with its four down-cards (see Appendix A). The flop is a bargain as well—three more cards for the price of one bet. Since you can see your first five cards after just two betting rounds, an expert will know at that point whether to continue or fold. Folding trouble hands after the flop is an essential art form in Hold'em.

Card Questions

How do you play Seven-Card Stud?
Each player is dealt two cards down and one face-up, followed by a betting round. Then three more cards are dealt face-up, with betting after each one, and then a last card (face-down) is dealt, followed by betting. The high card on the board bets first. There are no shared cards.

In Stud, Hold'em's chief rival for so many years, you see only four cards after two betting rounds. Stud is much slower, has an extra round of betting, and is more unpredictable. While your four individual board cards are a clue to your hand, with three down-cards you could have the worst mess of unmatched cards, and still conceal four of a kind. You are rarely completely safe from a ridiculous beat in Stud. In Omaha, because of the four-down cards and so many possible combinations against you, someone always seems to have the nuts, the worst-case scenario.

 Shark Bites

Poker legend Doyle Brunson on the variety and complexity of Texas Hold'em: "It has something for everybody . . . the mathematicians and psychologists . . . the 'loose gooses' and the 'hard rocks.'"

Hold'em is a thinking player's dream. You always know what the nut hand is, and the betting pattern is an easy clue to a player's holdings, even if you don't have time to study the player, his mannerisms, and his style of play. Knowing the nut hand gives the expert a chance to exploit those who don't realize when someone has a lock against him; the pro can quickly fold if he knows he's beat. While the good player will fold, others will call. The experienced player can also figure out from the play of the hand if she should fear the nuts, while lesser players either fear the nuts too much or not enough.

Fast Action

Skilled players, who feel they have an edge on every hand, want to play many hands. The more they play, the more they win, and Hold'em is a fast game. Casinos deal thirty hands or more an hour of Hold'em, more than Omaha and much more than Stud, which seems as though you're playing in quicksand. Online, you can be dealt sixty (or more) Hold'em hands per hour! For those waiting patiently for the rare, safe, and powerful premium hands to play, the more hands the better. This type of player is easy to spot. They always push the dealer to speed it up and hassle players who are taking their time. These "rocks" are low-level pros grinding out their "hourly rate," which usually amounts to about one big bet per hour ($8 in a $4–$8 game).

Hold'em is also perfect for the killer no-limit games that the old Texas rounders loved and that young players today are crazy for. Believe it or not, there are many new players today, skilled and unskilled, who only play no-limit! Many casinos are bringing no-limit back; and just a few years ago, it was difficult to find a no-limit game. Stud games, however, don't work well at no-limit.

More Edges

Hold'em can accommodate more players than any other game. It is best played with ten (versus eight with Stud), but it easily plays with more. Twelve-person games are common. In the early days, the Golden Nugget built a special table for fifteen. More players mean bigger pots (more money!) and more action, and since 71 percent of your cards are shared with others, the hands are very competitive.

Your position (see Chapter 5) stays constant in Hold'em, so you always know when you will act during a hand, unlike Stud games. Position can be a huge advantage (or disadvantage).

Texas Truths

With your hand linked to your opponents' hands through shared cards, it is much more difficult for someone to catch you if you are in the lead. Thus there are fewer of those shocking "bad beats" that good players dread, because if your opponent improves, you often will also.

Many players love the game because unlike Stud, you don't have to keep track of board cards or remember what cards have been folded. Instead, you can concentrate on strategy and reading players. Betting patterns are more important in Hold'em, while in Stud you must constantly relate a player's tells and betting to his individual board cards.

In Hold'em there is only one board, which makes it less of a gamble for the solid, everyday player—and more predictable, once you get to that level. Getting there takes a lot of experience and the ability to learn from every hand. Reading this book won't hurt either. Solid players don't want to gamble. They want the odds on their side.

Chapter 3
What Makes a Poker Player?

A successful player is smart, fearless, aggressive, patient, under control, without ego, focused, positive, always learning, analytical, and adaptable. Whew! And don't forget a comfortable bankroll! Looking for the opposite of these positive qualities is a way to spot a weak opponent. Yes, you do seek them out and exploit their weaknesses. You do not feel sorry for them. No one will take pity on you during your learning curve.

Poker Smarts

To win at the poker table, you must be smart—not just play smart. Aggressiveness and experience can make up for a lack of brainpower, but not totally.

Poker is difficult to play well and not just because you're risking something of value. You have to be sharp the whole time you're at the table: One missed signal and you could be lost. This is especially true in no-limit Hold'em, but also in limit games, when it takes a long time to dig out of a hole.

What It Takes

It's more than just knowing what the odds are of making a hand, of putting your opponents on hands (deducing from clues such as body language and playing style what hand they are holding), and what odds the pot is offering. It's split-second decision-making about a host of variables, and the dealers aren't going to wait around for you.

Besides being able to call up all your experiences with a hand over the years, and remember what you've read, and process that information with what your instincts are saying, you need to remember tells, clues, and the past performances of everyone at your table. Poker is much more than odds, as you'll soon find out. Like the old poker proverb says: "Poker isn't a card game played by people; it's a people game played with cards."

You must figure out what kind of person your opponent is and how he reacts in certain situations. Will he fold under pressure or welcome it? Does he bet on the come, slow-play, and/or a trap? Or is he a straight shooter? You must be a card player, risk-taker, mathematician, and psychologist. You have to be smart enough to learn from every hand. You need a solid memory, an understanding of the game, and the concentration to do it hand after hand, hour after hour.

A Poker Player Is Fearless

Poker is a test of courage. You're risking money, but it's so much more than that. There will be times when you have your *self* on the line alongside that cash. Walking into the poker room, sitting down with a bunch of strangers, making a bet, raising, folding, getting beat, raking a pot, you'll feel butterflies down to your toes the first time—and perhaps, every time.

Mastering your fear is mastering your inner self is mastering poker.

- You must be able to raise aggressively, and reraise.
- You must not be intimidated by more experienced players.
- You must stay strong if someone comes after you, with his chips or his mouth.
- You must not fear losing your money yet not be fool-hardy.
- You must not fear that someone has the nuts just because he raised you.
- You must not be afraid to fold a losing hand.
- You must not be afraid to fold a hand that might be a winner.
- You must not be afraid to wait patiently for a playable hand.

- You must not be afraid to bet all your chips with absolutely nothing.
- You must not be afraid to look a tough guy in the eye when you bluff.
- You must not be afraid to bet every cent on a hand (or a bluff) you believe in.
- You must believe in yourself, even if you're on a losing streak.

Being fearless means being confident and strong, no matter what the poker gods do to you.

Card Questions

What does it take to be a professional poker player?
Years ago, World Series of Poker champ and poker legend Amarillo Slim Preston was asked that question. "Well," he replied, "you have to have a strong constitution, and no nerves whatsoever."

A Poker Player Is Aggressive

Aggression is a winning strategy in part because if you bet often, no one is ever sure what you have. For now, just remember that aggression goes hand in hand with fear—not yours, theirs. Having others fear you and your hands is a major weapon. The best way to win pots is to have someone just give them to you without a fight.

Aggressive does not mean *reckless*. I am talking about controlled aggression—not rowdy, outrageous lunacy—combined with courage, intelligence, and instinct.

Aggression means making the most of your top hands by pressing your advantage, and taking control when you are in a hand and sense weakness. It doesn't mean playing poor cards. It does mean bluffing, semibluffing, buying pots, and trying to dominate the table. Aggression gives you so many more ways to win. It makes others react to *you*. It makes them guess and gives them the opportunity to guess wrong. Take the fight to the enemy. Beat them to the punch!

 Shark Bites

> Poker legend Doyle Brunson writes in *Doyle Brunson's Super System*: "You have to be extremely aggressive to be a consistent winner."

A Poker Player Is Patient

Know right now that you will get many, many more bad hands than good. And not all the good hands will win for you. You may wait for an hour or more before you get a Hold'em hand worth calling even one bet with, and then that hand may lose for you. Through it all, a good player patiently stays the course. He may examine his own play and the games he's been sitting in, but he does not question a strategy he knows is sound. He does not panic. And he definitely does not start playing poor starting hands to get in the action and recoup. Hoping to "get lucky" is a one-way ticket to Loserville. Trash hands just lose your money faster.

The good player has the discipline to sit for hours, folding bad hands. She will use her time to study players, make mental notes, and figure out how others perceive her (and who doesn't pay attention). When her image becomes super-tight, she can use it to steal some pots until the hands come.

Johnny Quads' Corner

In 1732 English churchman and historian Thomas Fuller wrote that "care and diligence bring good luck." While he was likely not speaking of poker, Fuller's advice holds true for the game. Instead of relying on chance, you can create your own luck through patient, solid play.

You absolutely must be patient during a losing streak and a horrible, interminable run of unplayable cards. Don't force it. You know the hands you want to play in each position against these specific opponents, and you must stick to your game plan. Just have faith that the bad streak will end, and realize that your profit comes from handling the streak better than your opponents would.

Play under Control

It's big-time Hold'em at Bellagio. You flopped a set (three of a kind) and are betting it up like crazy. It's a huge pot that will make you well. But some yo-yo catches two running spades (turn and river) to beat you. You can't believe it! What a night! You're as angry as John McEnroe at Wimbledon.

Do you blow your stack and rip his poor play or his intelligence? Absolutely not, that's a loser play. It feels good but costs you money. The last thing you want to do is make your loose-goose opponent mad. You want him sticking around. And you certainly don't want to clue him in that he played poorly.

So, you calmly muck your hand, take a sip of water, and get ready for the next hand. Sound tough? You bet it is. Nine out of ten players can't do it, and that's why nine out of ten are losers. Do you bet wildly the next hand on a prayer? No! You play your same solid brand of poker. Since he hit a 23-to-1 shot, the next time you expect to rake *his* chips.

Leave Your Emotions at Home

Letting your emotions warp your decision-making is the surest way to lose. In poker, you play because you think you have "the best of it"—the odds are in your favor—not because you are angry, envious, or want to defeat a particular player. Emotions suck reason and logic from your mind. Don't make these classic emotional mistakes at the table:

1. Calling a river bet because you're afraid of being bluffed out and that will make you look bad.
2. Calling with a drawing hand because the bettor is a jerk and you really want to beat him.
3. Taking it personally when someone raises you hand after hand, so you call with poor hands.
4. Taking a bad beat, and then letting your fury take over, throwing cards and berating the dealer or the player who beat you.
5. Taking a bad beat and then playing wild and loose to get it back, making obvious bluffs.

6. Playing against a particular player because of anger, envy, or fear, rather than playing your hand.
7. Playing angry, which squashes the reasoning part of your brain, the portion you need to play quality poker.
8. Instigating verbal confrontations with opponents, which will only make enemies and make you a target.
9. Letting bad players or jerks (and their comments) get to you. Either let your cards talk or leave.

Whining, complaining, or blaming rookies, the dealer, the cards, or the gods for your losses is weak and shows a lack of confidence, and lack of confidence is a sign of a loser. Good players are calm and in control. Take the good and the bad in stride, and don't ever let them see you sweat. Good players know they'll get it back.

"Keeping emotion out of it" doesn't mean you don't care. Of course, you care. But if you let your emotions play a part in your decisions, your decisions will be unsound, and you will lose.

 Texas Truths

The fact that fearless aggression must be combined with serenity and total emotional control is one of the paradoxes of poker.

Keep Your Ego in Check

Yes, you're confident. You believe in your ability, but walking around with a big ego will make enemies, and pride can cost you money. Remember, you're playing a game. You're playing to win, but your whole sense of self shouldn't be riding on it.

Some things to remember about the dangers of an inflated sense of self include:

- Ego is a cruel seductress who makes you play with emotion, not logic, with wishful thinking instead of your actual hand.
- Ego will trade you a flash of feel-good macho bravado for total ruin.
- Ego causes you to make plays based on factors other than the realities of the game at hand.
- Ego makes bluffers continue a bluff they know is futile.
- Ego makes a person who bet early keep betting even after it's clear he's beat.
- Ego makes someone who's been check-raised stay in a hand even though she knows she now has no chance.
- Ego makes you refuse to fold when an inferior player is raising, because you don't respect him. You lose.
- Ego makes you play too long when you're losing because you're "better than these guys." So, you lose big.

Ego and anger often travel together. "Why is that jerk raising my blind again? I'll show him," you growl as you fool-ishly toss in your chips, or reraise, with nothing. Don't make poker a turf war, unless, of course, you have the best of it.

Focused, Analytical, Adaptable, and Positive

If you're distracted, you give up a big edge to those who aren't. You cannot put the patterns, tells, and style of your opponents into your memory bank if you're spacing out. If you're not focused, you can't learn. Every hand should be a lesson about your opponents, the game, and the overall style you are developing. You also cannot take an analytical approach to the game if you are not sharp. Pay attention, even if you are not involved in the hand.

You are not at the table to throw chips around; you are there to win money, and don't ever forget it. To win, you need to be constantly analyzing the game, the players, and yourself, without seeming to do so.

From this strategy will come a positive feeling about yourself and your play. You focus on how much you think you'll win, not on how much you can afford to lose. You must believe you can win, but you also must approach each table dispassionately and analyze if this game is for you. Most players overrate themselves. You have to be honest enough to know when you're in a game you can't beat and have the courage to get up and leave.

Adaptability means you need to be able to change your style to maximize profit against particular players. There are games where guys are throwing chips around as if they've just won the lottery, and other games where nine Vegas retirees are just trying to make twenty bucks to supplement their Social Security and get a buffet comp. You should be able to recognize (and master) both, and everything in between, as well as adapt to the ever-changing nature of the game you're in and to the changing perceptions others have of you.

Johnny Quads' Corner

You know you've been at the table too long if someone you've been playing against for hours is suddenly gone, and you didn't even notice her leave. Or if there is a new face at the table, and you didn't see him sit down. Don't play on autopilot! Play alert.

Be Better Than Your Opponents

Know more about the game and the odds, be more observant, and keep improving your skills. Let others sit back smugly and think they're good—you keep learning. Their mistakes are your profits. If you're more skilled, you are the favorite, just like a minicasino with a built-in House edge. If you are the least skilled, you will have to get lucky to win, so be smart enough to find a new table.

Make More with Your Good Hands

When you have the best hand, bet it up; don't be afraid of the draws. Betting with the lead and making the chasers pay is one of the basic principles of good poker. Don't give opponents free chances to beat you. And if you believe you have the best hand, "value bet" it on the river to maximize your winnings.

Know When to Fold

Don't get married to a hand, no matter how good it is. Every hand except a royal flush has been beat. Don't pour chips into the pot when it's obvious you're facing a better hand.

The most obvious example is being raised by a player who never bluffs and rarely raises. Sure, she could be bluffing for the first time in her life, but do you want to bet on it? Discretion is definitely the better part of valor in poker, and playing cards destined to be second best is the quickest way to the poorhouse.

 Texas Truths

Folding is as much a skill as anything in poker. You make money by folding hands that inferior players would play (and lose with).

Choose Your Battles Carefully

Lose less with your bad hands. Just as understanding when to fold is an art form so is knowing which starting hands to play. Playing marginal hands drains your bankroll. You make money by facing trash hands mistakenly played by others, not by playing them yourself. Hands that start out second best usually end up second best.

Here's a quick Hold'em example: You're in the small blind and for just one-and-a-half more bets you decide to play 10-6 offsuit. The flop comes 10-9-3, and you're elated. You have top pair. You bet right out but are quickly raised, and another player calls the raise. You're likely facing some-one with tens with a higher kicker, like A-10, and probably a straight draw, too. You're stuck. Even the best you could reasonably hope for, pairing your high card and have it be top pair on the board, is not good enough. You're going to lose some money on a hand you shouldn't have played.

Be the Sharpest Hombre

This doesn't mean the sharpest dresser! It means being the most focused. If everyone is drinking at the table, be the least drunk. If everyone is tired at the table, be the least tired. If others are distracted, concentrate. If others are out of shape, get in shape. You can be one of the boys, or one of the girls, and still be smart. Small advantages add up in a big way, and these intangible factors can help you defeat players better than you.

Your Chips Are Golden

Even in a low-limit game, your chips (called "checks" by poker pros) are precious. Top players know that over time just one big bet per hour adds up to the difference between winning and losing. Don't make loose calls. Don't play long-shot hands in tight games. And especially don't throw in last bets on the river to keep someone honest if you know you're beat. Bets add up. Putting money in the pot should be the result of sound reasoning, not a whim.

Be Unpredictable

Vary your play to keep opponents guessing. Bluff early so that your good hands will be paid off, then start showing them only premium hands so they won't call when you start bluffing again. Tune in to how they perceive you at each moment. Create a table image to disguise your true nature and playing style.

Johnny Quads' Corner

It's easy to buy a car but very hard to sell one. That's a lot tougher. It's the same with your chips. They are easy to toss out into the pot but hard to get back.

Play at a Comfortable Limit

Feel good about the stakes. Look for games with people playing over their heads or with players coming down from a higher limit. Players who are over their head will be too timid, and high-limit refugees usually are unable to adapt and play too loose or not loose enough.

Be Friendly

Players mind losing to a nice guy a lot less than losing to a jerk. Making enemies at the table or trying to intimidate people with meanness is not a sound strategy. You don't want to be a target.

Of all the qualities you need to win at poker, there is one you really do not need to be, and that is lucky. As you will see in the next chapter, luck has little to do with it.

Chapter 4
A Game of Skill, Not Luck

Famous poker pro and lecturer Mike Caro used to always pose the question: "What is the object of poker?" If you've read this book carefully so far, you might answer, "To win money and have fun." But Caro believes that the object of poker is to make correct decisions. If you make the right decisions—based on your experience and knowledge of the game, not hoping for a lucky break—the other good things will follow.

Choose Your Poison

Unlike many other games of chance, in poker you have real strategic choices that can give you a positive expectation of winning. If you are playing a slot machine, the one-armed bandit's computer chip will be programmed to keep a certain percentage, usually 2 to 8 percent, over time. You may be fortunate and beat the machine in the short run, but you cannot change the House edge. If it is set to keep 5 percent, it will keep about five bucks out of every hundred dropped in the slot, and that is a big edge to overcome.

Of course, you might get lucky and hit a jackpot, but if you came to play, that money will start going back into the slot. Your only decisions are what to bet and when to pull the handle or hit the button. None of these choices will lessen the machine's advantage over you. (On progressive jackpot machines, playing the maximum allowable coins *will* decrease the House percentage because you qualify for the progressive prize pool.)

 Texas Truths

At a slot machine, you can easily play $100 in fifteen minutes, losing $20 an hour. In five hours, on average, it's gone. Slot players will tell you that a hundred can even disappear a lot quicker than that.

Oh Craps!

If you're shooting craps, the House has a mathematical advantage on every roll of the dice. You can decide which bets to make, and some are better than others, and you can decide how much to bet, but the House still has an edge on every wager. Unless you are one heck of a hunch player, the House percentage will take you down.

If you are a roulette junkie, and I pray you are not, you can choose which number, group of numbers, or color to bet, but it really doesn't matter. There is no real skill to it, only playing hunches and hoping to get lucky. The House has a huge 5.26 percent advantage on every single wager, and that is enough to make almost every player a loser. Maybe 5.26 percent doesn't seem like a lot to you, but it adds up. Remember, these seemingly small percentages built Las Vegas.

 Shark Bites

"For the true gambler, money is never an end in itself. It's a tool, like language or thought."
—Lancey in *The Cincinnati Kid*

Blackjack players say that with good basic strategy you can get to within a few percentage points of breaking even. If you can count cards and bet strategically, and the House deals far enough down into the deck (or decks), theoretically, you can achieve a slight edge. But casinos won't let you get that edge. They use multiple decks, and won't deal down far enough before reshuffling for you to get a serious advantage.

Still, if they even suspect you of card counting (in other words, playing the game intelligently), they will throw you out and bar you from the tables faster than you can yell, "That's not fair!" Casinos don't want winners at these table games, because your winnings come out of their pockets.

Vive la Difference!

But poker is different. You are not the pawn of an unflinching, whirling roulette ball or an indifferent, random roll of the dice. You are not playing against the House, with its inexorable edge, huge bankroll, and tremendous resources grinding you down on every bet.

To win over time in poker, you must simply be more skilled than the players you compete against. In other words, you must make better decisions. Their bad decisions (and your good ones) are where your profit is. You have choices, and your skills will force your opponents to make tough decisions, more of them than they want to, and many of those decisions will be based on guesswork, which will often be wrong. That means money flowing from their pockets into yours.

In poker, your choices have a very real effect on your expectation in a hand and in a game. Unlike House games like craps and roulette, where you can never gain an edge unless you are psychic, in poker you can gain a positive advantage through correct choices, and become, in a sense, your own casino, making money as if you were the House itself.

And the House doesn't care. You can win a bundle, or lose your last dime, and it won't matter either way to that powerful moneymaking behemoth. With poker all the House wants from you and the other players are your asses in the seats, so it can rake the pot, hand after hand, about thirty times an hour. The House takes a rake, or a percentage from each pot, which is what pays for the room, the drinks, the tables, the staff—everything. What cardrooms want is to keep the games running, so much so that they will even employ House players—not to win your money but to keep tables going if they become shorthanded.

 Texas Truths

A "shill" is a player paid an hourly wage by the House to start games or keep them from breaking up because there aren't enough players. Shills use House money, do not keep their winnings, and play tightly and passively.

Some rakes are more reasonable than others, but one thing is definite: you must be able to beat not only the other players but also the rake, or you will not win.

Beating the Rake

Even though you do not compete against the House at poker, the rake is still your enemy. A rake that is too high can suck you dry and insidiously eat up your bankroll and those of your tablemates and make it nearly impossible to win long term. Some rooms take 5 percent, which is fairly reasonable, and others take 10 percent, which is not. The rake should also have a cap. In low- and middle-limit games, a $3 cap is fair, $4 is all right, but $5 or more is too much.

What is important is not the percentage the House is taking but the percentage in relation to the average pot size. For example, if you are playing in a Florida poker room where the maximum bet is $2 and the rake is 10 percent up to a cap of $5, making a profit will be difficult. The average pot is about $40, so you'll pay 10 percent ($4); with the limit so low, you will be playing no-fold'em poker where you cannot use many of your skills. It's a crapshoot and the luckiest player will win instead of the best player.

 *Texas Truths*

A "proposition player" is paid by the House like a shill but plays with his own money and keeps his winnings. House players cannot check-raise and House personnel must identify them if asked. Prop players are more aggressive than shills.

The House takes four bucks a hand and the winner tips the dealer a buck, so at thirty hands an hour, $150 is taken out of play every sixty minutes. If ten players each buy in for $40, in just one hour, $150 of the $400 on the table will be in the House drop box—more than a third of all the money in play. You just can't beat that. A high rake is one reason you don't play limits that are too low; the pots rarely get big enough so that you are playing for nothing.

Compare that nightmare scenario to a desirable game, say $15–$30 limit Hold'em with a $4 cap. Whether the

House is taking the fair 5 percent or the unfair 10 percent is now irrelevant, because the average pot is $160 or more. That $4 House take amounts to only 2.5 percent. That's fair and beatable, the kind of rake you look for. After the $4 has been taken, you're freerolling.

 Johnny Quads' Corner

> Some Florida cruise ships sail past the three-mile off-shore limit (to avoid antigambling laws), then rake 10 percent up to $5, plus $2 (!) for a bad-beat jackpot, regardless of stakes. The game is impossible to beat, but that doesn't keep the suckers from trying.

A Different Kind of Rake

In higher-stakes games, most rooms will substitute a "seat charge" instead of raking each pot. This fee is about $9, depending on the game, and is collected every half hour. While the House usually makes more with a seat charge, the pots at these high-limit tables are so big that the seat charge can be beaten.

A Dealer's-Eye View

Dealers are frequently amazed at how many players are clueless about the rake. Some don't even know it exists. Others don't know how much they are paying or why. Others think it's for the dealer, which couldn't be further from the truth. To the cardroom, the dealer's chief job is to keep raking the pot because it all goes right into the House till. Dealers survive almost solely on tips, and dealing is no picnic. These working stiffs are just trying to make a living, so don't treat the dealer as an enemy. You are much better off treating him or her as a friend. After all, why would you want to alienate the person who is handling the cards and running the game? It's not the dealer's fault if you take a bad beat or have a run of bad cards. He's not stacking the deck.

Card Questions

What are "snatch" games?
Back in the Mob days of Vegas, some rubes were so clueless about the rake and the size of the pot that dealers not only took the rake but also grabbed bunches of chips from pots through some not-so-subtle sleight of hand. Thankfully, you won't find this in casinos anymore.

If you can't afford to tip the dealer a buck, you have to ask yourself if you can afford the game. Just think of it as part of the cost of doing business, so give the dealer his due. If you only won the blinds or a few bucks and that dollar is crucial to you, then keep it. But if the dealer has bailed you out on the river with a miracle card, give her a nice toke. After all, your play didn't win that hand, the dealer's miracle card did. And if you've won a huge pot, cast your bread upon the waters in a big way.

Some pro wannabes claim that professional players don't tip. This is not true. Yes, most everyday grinders watch their bottom line and are not huge tokers relative to the size of their pots, but they still give a buck. They realize that if you plan to play in a room every day, you don't want the staff, and your fellow players, to think you're too cheap, miserly, penny-pinching, and selfish to share a bit with the person who dealt you a winner. If you planned to eat in the same restaurant again, you wouldn't stiff the wait-staff, would you?

Players who don't tip upset the other players as well as the dealer. It's a break in protocol that sets everyone on edge. It is also a tell that you may be playing with scared money, or that you are an online player who is not used to real flesh-and-blood Hold'em. You don't want to give this kind of info away. So make it a habit: you win a pot, then you toss the dealer a buck. Everybody's happy.

 Texas Truths

You won't find it in any poker-math book, but there's something to be said for good karma and being generous at the table. Nice people seem to be winners, while whiners and skinflints seem to lose.

Is Poker Gambling?

There's always somebody who says poker is all luck. Usually it's someone who is losing at the game (or a mis-guided relative). In the sense that the outcome of every hand is uncertain, you might call it gambling. That uncertainty gives inferior players hope. There is luck involved in every hand, if you mean the random fall of the cards. But if you are more skilled than your foes, part of that skill is to know the odds. If you get the odds on your side, the immutable laws of math can go a long way toward making you a winner. Combine that with greater skill at reading players and other strategies, and you will find it not only fairly easy to win but also difficult to lose.

Johnny Quads' Corner

You might say that while every hand is a gamble, the long-term result of a skilled player is anything but.

Take this example. You've seen circus performers shot out of a cannon. It's not an illusion. It's dangerous. But for the expert who has done it thousands of times and is well-trained and has meticulously calculated the distance and his weight and calibrated and tested the machine and double-checked everything, it's an impressive feat that is such a sure thing that he can do it in front of an audience of kids. Is there a chance that something will go wrong and he'll miss that net when he comes down? Of course, there is, so in that sense it's a gamble. For the expert, however, it's a calculated risk, and a whole sequence of bad things has to occur for him to get hurt.

But for you, the person who knows nothing about cannons, it would be a gamble—probably a losing one. You'd be "lucky" to survive. For the expert human cannonball, on the other hand, it's almost a sure thing. The same holds true when you are an expert at the poker table, your calculated risks will pay off, especially if you play against those who must rely on luck to win. You may not hit that net every time (win every game), but when you know what you're doing, you are a big favorite to win long term and probably short term as well.

Since it is conceivable that something crazy could happen, like someone flipping 100 heads in a row on a fair coin, or you missing every flush draw for the rest of your life, you could consider poker gambling. But casinos make millions on less of an edge than you can get playing Hold'em.

Lucky Streaks

Sometimes, no matter how perfectly you play on a given night, you will not win. The best poker players in the world have gone broke. But over time, the quality of your cards evens out. You will get about the same number of good and bad hands as everyone else. It's how you play them that will decide if you are a winner or a loser, and what you do with your bad hands is just as crucial as how you play your good ones. Over time, if you are trying to hit a 4-to-1 flush draw on the river, you will hit it about one out of five times. In any given hand, hitting the draw is a gamble, but long term, you can rest assured that you will make it the expected 20 percent of the time.

Deviant Behavior

Make no mistake, streaks of good and bad outcomes exist. They are part of the mathematical equation. You might miss that draw twenty straight times. This is called deviation; you might call it bad luck. It can drive players crazy over the short term, but as sure as water runs downhill, with enough hands, the deviation will approach the expected result.

That is not to say that just because you've missed ten flush draws in a row, you are due to hit the next one. The cards have no memory, anymore than a roulette ball does. Your odds of hitting that flush are still 4 to 1 no matter what has gone before, and in roulette, the chance of hitting red are the same even if black has come up ten times in a row on a fair wheel.

Take a Spin

Look at any roulette wheel in a casino. There is a tote board listing the last twenty or thirty spins. On almost every one, you will see a group of five black or five red spins in a row. Even though the odds against this would seem quite high, these runs are, in fact, quite common.

Five blacks or five reds, over time, will occur once out of sixteen groups of five roulette spins. That streak is just as expected and mathematically proven as the seemingly more logical alternation of red and black. A Hold'em player who needs trips to win is going to hit one of his two winning cards once out of twenty-three tries. But you don't want to bet that this will be that time. In most cases, you want to be the favorite, betting that someone *won't* get that miracle card. Let her do the praying. You won't need to.

What people call luck is just randomness, and randomness is controllable over time with sound play that puts you in a position to make your own luck.

Shark Bites

World Poker Tour millionaire Gus Hansen says that "a good understanding of the structure of the game creates its own 'luck.'"

Playing the Odds

Good players possess two chief skill sets: the mathematical and the psychological. The psychological helps you divine patterns and weaknesses in your foes, while the mathematical provides your chance of winning, whether your hand is a favorite or a longshot, and how much money to invest. Without the math, you cannot make the correct decisions, even if you could see your opponents' cards.

Every hand has potential. Some hands have a high profit factor, like pocket kings, while some will always be money losers, like 3-2. Expectation varies depending on the type of game you're in and how many opponents you expect will be playing the hand. In lower-limit games, you need a good hand at the showdown because you are going to be called. In high-limit and no-limit contests, every hand has potential because the games are less about the cards and more about betting, aggressiveness, guts, and reading players.

Figuring Potential

Being able to "put people on hands" will help you figure your hand's potential. If you believe you have the best hand, you will often be betting it up. Usually, if you are the best hand, you are the favorite to win the hand, even if you have only seen your first two cards or the flop. Sometimes, if there is a very large field against you, you might be an underdog. In that case, you might bet to try to force some folds. If your hand is trailing but has a chance to be best at the showdown, as with a nut flush draw, then you might bet. Figuring odds lets you know your chances and whether that chance is worth a bet, a raise, a call, or a fold.

Texas Truths

Based on earning power, the top twenty Hold'em start-ing hands are aces, kings, queens, jacks, A-Ks, tens, A-K, A-Qs, K-Qs, A-Js, A-10s, A-Q, nines, K-Js, K-Q, K-10s, A-9s, A-J, eights, Q-Js ("s" means suited). The chance of getting a top-twenty hand out of the 169 possible: 9.5 percent.

Odds Are

Generally, you don't want to be on the chasing side of the odds. You want to be the favorite and press the action, and you want to start with hands that have a positive expectation of making money. How you play the hand affects your expectation, of course, but to give you a general idea, pocket aces are an 88 percent favorite heads-up but only win a third of the time against nine random hands if all stay to the river. Pocket eights are 71 percent heads-up, only 16 percent against a full table at the river. Pocket deuces are 55 percent heads-up, but only 10 percent against a table full of random hands.

A-Q (ace-queen) offsuit wins 39 percent of hands against three random hands playing to the river, 19 percent against nine players. 10-9 is 27 percent versus three players, 10 percent against nine. 3-2 is 14 percent against three players, 3 percent against nine. (Suited hands fare about 3 percent better.) Note that these percentages assume "playing to the river." It is up to you to make these hands fold *before* the river if you are leading in order to protect your hand from the longshots.

Finding Your "Outs"

"Outs" are the cards in the deck that will help your hand, and it is essential that you know how many you have at all times. If you are in the lead, you must be aware of your chance of improving—and of your opponents' chances. If you have A♠-J♥and the flop comes A♣-J♣-10♠, you have two pair, easily the best hand now. Based on the betting and your knowledge of your foe, you do not believe he has a K-Q for a straight, but you think you are facing a high-card type, so there is a straight draw out there. If he has a king or queen, he has only four outs—a longshot. However, someone with A-K has seven outs: three kings for a higher two pair and four queens for a straight. Someone with A-K, both clubs, has three kings, three queens that are not clubs, and nine remaining clubs (for a flush) for outs—that's fifteen! Fifteen outs give your foe a 54 percent chance of hitting his hand (see the table on pages 118–119). If he hits, the only way you win is to hit one of your four outs: the two aces and two jacks you must assume are still in the deck.

Texas Truths

Odds are a ratio. If you have one chance in five of hitting your hand, your odds are 4-to-1 against, often stated as 4-1. Probability is your chance relative to the total chances, as in "1 out of 5" or "1 in 5." Probability is frequently expressed as a percentage: 20 percent.

Pot Odds: An Essential Tool

One of the most important concepts in limit poker is pot odds. This tool will guide you when all else fails. In Hold'em, you must always be aware of the pot size, and the easiest way is to keep track of how many bets are in there. Count the small bets during the first two rounds, and convert them to big bets on the turn and the river. (If you're playing $5–$10, $5 is the small bet and $10 is the big bet.)

You don't want to be chasing all the time—an underdog going for straights and flushes that usually won't get there—but is it ever right to go for them? You bet! You chase when you are getting proper odds from the pot.

An Example

Say you have 8♦-7♦ and the flop is Q♠-J♦-2♦. You need one more diamond for a flush. There are nine left in the deck out of forty-seven unseen cards (you have subtracted the flop and your two hole cards from fifty-two). You must assume the diamonds are still in the deck, not in someone's hand, because you just don't know. So, the odds against you making a flush on the turn are 38-9. Simplified (divide by 9), that's about 4-to-1.

Johnny Quads' Corner

In a ten-person game, if you have an ace, there is a 75 percent probability someone else does too. If you don't have an ace, there is an 84 percent chance someone has one. In five-handed, the likelihood is 41 percent and 51 percent.

If someone has bet $5 into your four-flush, and if there is more than $20 in the pot, you can call. Ideally, you want more than 4-to-1 odds from the pot, to make up for those times when someone beats you with a higher flush or you make your flush but the board pairs and someone beats you with a full house. Remember, if there is a raise, you may no longer have the proper odds to call. If you don't make your flush on the turn, there is still the river, when you will have another pot-odds decision. If you had the odds to call on the turn, you will usually have them on the river as well, unless there is a lot of raising.

If you want to know your odds with two cards to come, just divide your 4-1 odds by two. Your 2-1 estimate is pretty good. This is useful if you are going all-in after the flop and don't have to worry about a bet after the turn.

Another Example

There is one card to come. You have top two pair and need to fill up to beat the flush you are sure someone has. You have only four outs out of forty-six unseen cards for odds of 42-4, or 10.5-1. The bet is $10 to you, and there is $70 in the pot. You don't call because the pot is only offering you 7-to-1. Don't be a sucker. If your local bookie offered you 7-1 odds on a horse that should be a 10-1 longshot, you wouldn't take it—so don't take it from the pot. But if the pot contains $140, you'd be getting 14-to-1, so jump in. You won't make it very often, but when you do, it will be worth it. And more important, over the long term, if you make all your bets overlays (when you are paid off more than the proper odds dictate) like this, you will be on your way to making a bunch of cold, hard cash. Plays like this give you a very real edge.

A Paradox

There are times when the chaser and the player with the best hand are both correct to pursue the hand. For example, you have A♠-Q♥ and the board is A♦-9♦-4♣-3♣. Your lone remaining opponent has J♦-10♦ for a flush draw with nine outs. He's a 4-1 underdog (20 percent). You're a 4-1 favorite (80 percent). Of course, you would bet your firstborn here, but since you're playing $5–$10 limit poker, you can only bet $10. If he calls, you are getting even money on your bet when you should be giving 4-1 odds. But your foe sees that there is $60 in the pot, so he correctly calls. He's getting 6-to-1. You're both right.

Who, then, was wrong? Well, no matter who wins, your profit will come from those players who put money in the pot early but who have since dropped out. There is a lesson here: Be careful which hands you play. You don't want your bad decisions early in a hand to be someone else's profit.

And since some of that $60 belongs to you and your opponent, and not just the folded players, at times you will be stuck calling on the river because of earlier bad play. Make sure you have a solid reason or the math going for you before you call bets early in a hand. They could come back to haunt you.

 Texas Truths

Avoid chasing draws against only one player. You won't hit very often, and you won't make much when you do.

Implied Pot Odds

Let's say that in the previous example, you think that because there is a flush out there and maybe a straight also, if you hit your full house, a full-scale raising war could break out. You need $105 in the pot just to break even on that $10 call, but you figure you can get at least $20 each off two opponents, maybe more, if you hit. With $70 in the pot plus another $40, that's $110 for "implied odds" of 11-1. It's a doable bet—barely. Implied odds assume action after you hit, so know your players and how obvious your monster hand will be when you hit. Flushes are easy to spot, and a river card pairing the board is a red flag. Straights are better hidden. Just be careful you don't use implied odds to justify loose play. Folding is always a viable option with a chasing hand. There's no shame in it.

Johnny Quads' Corner

Don't use money you have invested in a hand as an excuse to stay in the hand. The money in the pot is no longer yours. If you stay in the hand, it should be for sound reasons, not because you tossed in a lot of chips in previous rounds.

Betting Odds

These are separate from pot odds and are used in an advanced play by aggressive players. Betting odds situations often occur with a large field. Say you have a nut flush draw with A♥-10♥ after a ragged flop (three mismatched cards under ten) of 9♥-5♥-2♣ and are facing six players who love to gamble. You are a 4-1 underdog to hit on the turn, but if you bet and they all call, you're getting 6-to-1 on your bet. That's a good bet! (If they all call, of course.) Some players push it a step farther and say that since they are only a 2-1 dog (35 percent) to make the flush by the river, as long as they are getting more than 2-1, they are making a good bet.

If you like to bet it up and don't mind short-term losses, this play is for you. Just remember, it could easily put you in the hole. You're still an underdog, no matter how big the pot is. Having the nut draw is best for this type of play; if the board pairs, your flush is no longer the best-possible hand.

Odds Become Second Nature

It's a good idea to deal out hands at home, practice doing simple odds problems in your head, and study the charts later in the book. After a while, many of the decisions rooted in odds will become automatic. Keep in mind that odds are just the beginning of your poker knowledge, not the end.

Card Questions

Is it true that if you go with the math on every decision, you cannot lose in the long run?
No. While many mathematical players would answer yes, this is misguided. There is much more to poker than percentages, and there are many situations where math will not help you.

For example, a Hold'em board is A-9-9-9-2. You have pocket aces. Your conservative foe has been raising you on the flop, the turn, and now the river. There is only one card she can have that will beat your aces-full—the case nine. That's just one out of the forty-five unseen cards. The odds against her having it are 44-to-1. But you know in your head, based on the player and the betting, that it wouldn't matter if it's a million to one—she's got the case nine! As the old-school players say, "The odds are fifty-fifty. Either he's got it, or he don't!"

Playing the odds are your training wheels. Getting the best of it complements guts and reading players and your other poker skills, but it is not a substitute for them or a cure for a lack of them.

As with the coin-flip, probability needs time to work. You may hit that flush draw on the river two times in a row, or you may miss it ten times straight. Over the years, you have to believe that you will hit it the expected percentage of the time. Make the right decision and don't look back.

Chapter 5
Get Position, Isolate, and Trap

Poker, being a game of decisions, is all about information. The more you know about your opponents and the cards they hold, the more correct decisions on betting, calling, raising, and folding you will make. Good choices make money, and playing "position" is a monster advantage in the hunt for information in Hold'em, more so than in any other form of poker. You can use that knowledge to find weakness and to isolate the player like a lion attacking a wounded wildebeest.

The Essence of Position

In Hold'em, you can go from rags to riches with lightning speed during a hand, but one thing you can count on is your position. It is constant throughout the hand. Action always starts to the left of the dealer, so if you are up-front, you will have to reveal your intentions (and often the value of your hand) first. If you are near the button, you can sit back and evaluate the sumptuous buffet of information your opponents spread before you by the ways they check, bet, call, or raise.

Say you limped into the pot on the button (as the dealer) against four foes with Q♥-8♥, and the flop is Q♠-9♦-4♣. You have a pair of queens with a weak kicker, a borderline hand. But if everyone checks to you, you can bet it and probably take the pot. In fact, in late position, you can bet no matter what cards you have in this situation because everyone else has shown weakness. It would be the same if the flop was A♠-Q♦-4♣. If everyone checks to you, you bet, even though the scary ace is out there. The players have told you all about their hands with their actions or lack of them. If there is a bet to you or a bet and a raise (in either example), you can cheaply fold with no harm done.

 Texas Truths

The more players acting before you, the greater your positional advantage is. Their checks and bets usually tell you everything you need. All that's left is for you to know them well enough to divine if anyone is being deceptive.

Now compare this fortunate scenario to one in which you are in an early position. You are the first to act with a hand that may be best but can very easily cost you a bundle. If you check, you show weakness and invite a bet. If you bet, and then you are raised, you must fold the hand. You are beat, and you just wasted some chips because Q-8 is not a viable hand to play in early position. If someone just calls you, you still might be beat. On the next round, you will have to act first again. If you bet, you could be raised, or you may be betting on a loser all the way to the showdown. If you check, you invite a rout by showing weakness.

Position Play

Before the flop in a typical ten-person game, if you are one of the three players to the left of the blinds, you are in early position. The next three players are in middle position, and the dealer and the person to the right of the button are in late position. The blinds act last before the flop, first after it. After the flop, the first third of the remaining combatants are in early position, the next third are in middle position, and the remaining third are in late position. The later your position is, the less chance there is of someone having better cards than you, and the less chance there is of someone having a monster hand.

Early Position

Early position is the poker equivalent of twisting slowly in the wind. You have no information to work with, and you must be the first to give some away. This is the opposite of where you want to be.

Position is a huge factor in your decision on whether to play or fold every hand in your Hold'em life. As you will learn next chapter, certain draw-type starting hands, such as 8-7 suited, cry out for a large field to get that big payday when they finally hit, but they are not worth calling raises with. They are just too speculative in a game dominated by high cards, such as Hold'em. So, many of these hands must be folded in early position because you do not yet know the size of the field or if there will be raises after you act.

 Johnny Quads' Corner

If you are in early position, you do not want to play a lot of hands because you have little information to help you and only stand to reveal clues about your hand to your opponents.

As the button nears, there is less chance of a raise. You can play more hands. While K-10 may be very playable in late position, it is too risky in early position because if there is a raise or two after you, you cannot call with this hand. There is just too much chance that it is "dominated," because hands like A-K, A-Qs, K-Q, A-10, and high pocket pairs are just the types of hands that kill K-10, and these are exactly the hands that people raise with. If you are facing one of these hands, you will often have only three outs. You are more than a 3-1 dog to A-K, 9-1 to K-K, and 2-1 to A-Qs.

Card Questions

What is a dominated hand?
If you have A-K and some poor sap has A-Q, or you have K-J and he has Q-J, you have him dominated. You have a card in common, but your other card—your "kicker"—is higher. Only three cards in the deck will save him.

Early position is weak. During later rounds, you must check some marginal hands—hands that you might bet or bluff with in late position after others have shown weakness. Since you're first, you don't have this luxury.

Middle Position

In middle position, you are literally caught in the middle. How you play the middle position depends on the type of game. If it's a raise-fest, you must fold many hands as if you were in early position. If you're in a passive game, you can play some more of those speculative hands (10-9, 8-7 suited, 5-5) that want to limp into a large field. In an average game, these are late-position hands.

If you don't believe that, think what your reaction would be if you limped in with 9-8 expecting some weak limpers to call behind you and the blinds to check. Instead, you get a raise or two. Now you must fold. If you decide to gamble, you could find yourself facing just one or two opponents after the smart players have folded. You have invested a lot of money and are stuck with a hand you know is inferior. You will have to get very lucky to win, and you won't win much if you do.

Johnny Quads' Corner

Sit "behind the money." Try to position yourself so that the players with the most chips are on your right. That is where the power is, and if they are raising, you will know it before you call bets. Besides, money seems to flow clockwise in a Hold'em game.

Late Position

While you are stuck in molasses in early position, late position is a breeze. You have studied the players in front of you as they called and raised, and you should have a good idea of their strength. You know the size of the field and whether there have been raises. You can easily evaluate if your starting hand is playable. Postflop, you will have the same advantages. You will be able to smell the flop-sweat from those with borderline hands who fear a raise if they bet. Don't disappoint them.

If you are one or two spots to the right of the button, try "buying the button" if you decided to enter the hand preflop. Just raise it, and the hands after you that might have been on the fence will probably fold. Now you will be the last to act during the hand. If there has already been a raise, making it two bets to go is a surefire way to thin the field. Only the loosest players or those with killer hands will call two raises cold.

The Free Card

Getting a free card is a time-honored play by good players in late position. If someone in front of you has bet after the flop and you have a good draw (nut flush or open-ender) that you know you will take to the river, go ahead and raise. Your opponent will just call (unless she has an absolute monster). After the turn, she will check to you. You check right back if you didn't make your hand. You've now saved that more expensive bet on the turn and received a chance to draw at the nuts for free.

There is a more aggressive way of playing the free card. If you sense weakness after your raise on the flop, bet it strongly on the turn no matter what card hits the board. You may be able to buy the pot right there, or with another strong bet on the river. You've taken control and they probably will put you on a made hand.

Stealing the Blinds

If you are in late position, raising to steal the blinds if no one has called or raising to get the blinds out of the hand is a classic Hold'em strategy. The blinds are vulnerable. Their money was out there before they'd even seen their cards. Since most hands in Hold'em are unplayable, a bet into the blinds makes sense. And thinning the field is rarely a bad move. If they call your raise, unless you have these players pegged as loose gooses, you know they have something. This is critical information for formulating your postflop strategy.

Make the Blinds Pay!

Letting the blinds limp in can be suicide for good hands. Unless you've got a killer hand like pocket aces, kings, maybe queens, maybe A-K, and no one has called, get those blinds out or make them pay. With those rare monster pocket pairs (getting pocket rockets is a 220-to-1 shot), you want to get some payoff. Forcing the blinds out is a mistake. But if some players have already limped in and you have what you think is the best hand, such as the ones mentioned or pocket jacks, A-Q, K-Qs, and the like, or any hand you think is worth a late-position raise, by all means raise it. Force the blinds out!

Johnny Quads' Corner

Don't forget, your foes might be on draws also. If they're weak, keep firing. If you force them to fold, your four-flush is now a winner. Betting a draw on the turn can be a winning play.

The Hold'em graveyard is littered with late-position premium hands like A-J suited that went down in flames when the flop came J-6-4 and the blinds were let in cheap and flopped two pair with some trash like J-4 or 6-4. Raising takes the guesswork out and keeps these freak hands from beating you. If you let the blinds in without a raise, no flop is safe. Anything could happen.

If you have A-Q or A-10 in late position with this flop, and one of the blinds bets right out, you will have a hard time calling. Even if a blind has only a pair of fours, you have six outs to pair up—a 25 percent chance with two cards to come.

A Blind Mistake

Many rocks playing old-school book strategy make a serious mistake in the blinds in loose games. If you are the small blind and the pot is not raised and five, six, or more players limp in preflop, putting in that half a bet is essential. If five players are in, you are getting paid 11-to-1 on that half bet. There aren't too many start hands that aren't worth 11-to-1! With six players, you're talking 13-to-1. Seven players, 15-to-1!

If you are the big blind facing a single raise and you are sure no more raises are coming, and there are seven players in, you're also getting 15-to-1 on your money. How can you not call this?

Hanging by a Thread

It's a long way home in Hold'em, and even the best starting hands are vulnerable. Let's face it, you're only seeing two of your seven cards before you have to put money at risk. Seventy-two percent of your hand is still unknown. The game can be extremely unpredictable; the more hands out there that are against you, the greater chance that you will get an unpleasant surprise in the form of someone getting lucky. Pocket aces, for example, are an overwhelming 88 percent favorite against one player, but against a full table, they only win a third of the time. Lowly deuces take the pot 55 percent of the time against one player (only higher pocket pairs have them dominated) but are a money-draining 10 percent against a full field (see the following table).

The table shows the winning percentage for some pocket pairs against differing numbers of random hands when all stay to the river. You will wind up with a set about 20 percent of the time. You'll flop a set one out of 8.5 tries (12 percent).

Pocket Pairs Versus Multiple Opponents

Players	Pocket Pairs					
	AA	QQ	TT	88	55	22
2	88	82	77	71	63	55
4	68	58	50	43	33	22
7	44	34	27	23	19	15
10	34	26	20	16	12	10

Note: Tables like this are a general tool. You face random hands in the simulation, but in actual play, the hands will be better than random. The betting, of course, changes everything, because while in the simulation everyone plays to the river, in actual practice this isn't the case.

Fear Multiple Opponents

It is imperative that you decide what type of starting hand you have in Hold'em. If you are dealt a drawing hand, like suited connectors (9♥-8♥) and low pairs (4♠-4♦), you usually want a large field, but these hands are the exception. Most of the time, you do not want to be chasing. You want the power, and in Hold'em, power hands fear a large field. You want to thin the field to protect the hand, and often to isolate—get it heads-up against a weaker player and/or weaker holding.

Sooner or later, you'll be tempted to get greedy. You'll try to suck some players into the pot with pocket kings or queens to get a big payoff. Instead of raising and reraising, you'll let someone in with A-6 offsuit or A-2, and then when an ace flops, of course, you bet, but it's too late. Getting a third king is an 11-1 longshot. You're going to lose a lot of chips.

Card Questions

What is an "overcard"?
It is a higher card than what you hold. If you have pocket kings and the flop is A-6-2, an overcard has hit the board. The ace is an overcard to your kings. If you have pocket nines and the flop is 8-5-3, you have an "overpair" to the board.

An Enemy Army

You cannot treat your opponents as individuals; you must look at them collectively as an enemy force out to destroy you. It doesn't matter if your pocket jacks are the best hand preflop, you want to be favored to win against all the other hands combined; that's how you win money. And as the previous table shows, even pocket aces are vulnerable against a large enough fighting force. This is why no-limit tournament players bet so aggressively: They don't want multiple opponents; in fact, they usually don't want to be called at all. They're happy just to take a smallish pot rather than risk playing to the river. In limit Hold'em, you want a payoff with your great starting hands, but you don't want a bunch of callers. A few to pay you off will be good enough. As you descend from pocket aces, the more tenuous your lead becomes, and the fewer players you want calling you.

Overcard Obstacle

The problem with hands such as pocket queens, jacks, tens, and nines and A-J suited when the flop is J-9-8 is first one of overcards. They are murder in this game. If they don't beat you, they slow you to a crawl. Anyone with a king or queen could pair up on the turn or river and beat you with an overpair to your jacks.

If you let a bunch of players limp into the pot because you didn't raise, this is a scary flop. Someone could have played trash like 10-7 and now has a straight. Someone could have a ten for an open-ender. Anyone with J-9, J-8, or 9-8 has two pair and you're beat. Even if you have the lead now, and being optimistic, let's assume that your only worries are a king, queen, or ten on the turn or river, there are still ten outs against you. The enemy will draw out on you 38 percent of the time. If there is two of a suit on the flop, someone might have a four-flush and nine more outs against you.

Thin the field to avoid surprises and ugly scenarios like this. Raise aggressively preflop with power hands.

Pocket Pair Dilemma

Pocket pairs are especially at risk. With pocket queens, there is a 31 percent chance that there will be an overcard on the flop (and you haven't flopped a set). Since aces and kings are the cards most people play, you are probably beat if one flops. With jacks, it's 47 percent; with tens, it's 60 percent.

Johnny Quads' Corner

You must either force players to fold before the flop with these hands or not play them at all. If you're a defeatist, you can limp with pairs, queens, and below into a large field and pray for a set or three undercards, but this is weak.

The problem is that if you believe someone has a higher pair on the flop, you have only two outs to win if you have a pocket pair, or an 8 percent chance. If you have paired a hole card against a likely overpair, such as K-J with a flop of A-K-2, then you have five outs (20 percent). If you believe someone has an overpair, it is very difficult to call his bet. However, if you have thinned the field by betting aggressively, and perhaps have isolated your hand against a single foe, then if you have pocket jacks and the flop is A-10-7, K-Q-4, or Q-9-7, your hand might still be good. But against multiple opponents, you're finished. Someone's paired up.

Remember that you're only going to pair a hand like A-K about three out of ten tries on the flop. If someone has paired a hole card on the flop, and you haven't, you are more than a 3-1 dog, with only six outs. But if you've isolated, this hand can still win unimproved, because your opponent likely hasn't paired either and you've taken control of the hand by raising preflop.

Your opponent might put you on a high pocket pair. Another advantage is that by isolating, you may have denied any drawing hands the proper pot odds to call.

Since a single opponent will miss the flop most of the time, if you've aggressively gotten it heads-up with position, all it will take is a flop bet to make her fade into the sunset.

Chance of Overcards on the Flop

You Have	None	1 or More	Overcard(s) & No Set If Paired
1 or 2 kings	77%	23%	12%
1 or 2 queens	59%	41%	31%
1 or 2 jacks	43%	57%	47%
1 or 2 tens	31%	69%	60%
1 or 2 nines	21%	79%	69%
1 or 2 eights	13%	87%	77%
1 or 2 sevens	8%	92%	82%
1 or 2 sixes	4%	96%	85%
1 or 2 fives	2%	98%	87%
1 or 2 fours	.6%	99%	88%
1 or 2 threes	.1%	99%	88%
1 or 2 twos	--	100%	88%

Note: The column on the right shows the probability of the flop containing at least one overcard when you have a pocket pair, and you do not flop trips. In other words, the likelihood that the flop will hurt you.

Who to Isolate

Here are the prime candidates to try to get one-on-one whenever possible by aggressive preflop play. The first is the "calling station"; this player loves to see flops and he rarely raises. He sees so many flops so passively that you know he's limping in with many mediocre holdings. Get him alone whenever possible with your better hand. Force him out after the flop when he misses.

Wild players, or "maniacs," are tailor-made for your isolation strategy. These players are always raising preflop with questionable cards. Build on their raises by making it two bets to go, and most players will fold. Once heads-up, you can be pretty sure you have the better hand. A raise on the flop by a maniac rarely means anything.

Players who are steaming because of bad plays, bad cards, and bad beats are often just throwing their chips away in a vain, kamikaze effort to get back to even. They play questionable cards and have lost all sense of reason.

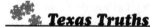

Texas Truths

The players you don't want to isolate: solid early-position raisers and callers, and ultratight players. These players may have real hands they'll take to the river, no matter what.

Novice players don't understand heads-up play and don't realize you may be making a move. Figure out if your rookie opponent understands the game and is the type to play only ultrapremium starting hands, or if she will call preflop raises with cards that look good but are actually borderline, like Q-9 or A-7. Will she go to the river to keep you honest, or can she be chased out after the flop? Is she capable of laying down a hand? Either way, isolating an inexperienced player can never be a bad tactic.

This brings us to straddlers. In a straddle, a player puts up a "third blind" that is twice the big blind. If the big blind is $4, he puts up $8—before he has even seen his cards! The straddle is "live:" He will have the option to raise, and he often does. The straddle is used by pot-building action players, but it is one of the most foolish moves in Hold'em. In a ten-person game, he's raised in the dark with 9-1 odds of winning the hand. What kind of loon raises without seeing his cards? Try to get it heads-up with any above-average hand.

Setting a Trap

Since keeping information from your opponents is vital to winning, misdirection and deception are essential weapons in your arsenal. Opponents must know that you will not always play the same hand the same way and that you will set traps for them. Sometimes you will play pocket kings fast (raising and reraising), while other times you may lie in the weeds and call, feigning weakness. While straightforward play is a good way to start your career, being honest makes you predictable, and that is no way to win. If three cards to a flush hit the flop (10♦-8♦-4♦), sometimes bet if you hit the flush, and other times check. If you don't have a flush, sometimes bet anyway. Sometimes bet with a four-flush, other times don't.

The Fine Art of Slow-Playing

If you flopped a flush in the earlier example and checked it, hoping to induce a bet, you are trapping. Although if you bet right out, many players may believe you and put you on a flush and fold; if you check, aggressive players may bet into your weakness and try to buy the pot or bet their single pairs as if they were good. You sit back, maximize your profits, and hit them with check-raises when the time is right, usually on the big-bet later rounds.

Realize that with your greater profit comes greater risk. If your flush was with the 9♦-8♦, you are vulnerable. There's a one in three chance of a diamond hitting on the turn or river, and if someone has a diamond higher than your nine, you lose. Hands with the ace or king of diamonds are just the hands that players will see the turn and river with in this situation. Slow-playing here is much more prudent if your flush contains the king or ace.

You Must Check-Raise

The check-raise is an essential weapon, and not just because it often makes you more money, but because it sends a message. First, you tell the table you're a serious player who came to win. You're not there to be nice.

Second, you tell the table that when you check, it doesn't necessarily mean you are weak. If you check, you could be sitting there with a big hand that will blow up in their faces if they try to run over you. You are not always what you appear to be. You are an unknown, a scary player, someone not to be messed with. You have gained power; others will have to guess about your future hands, and guessers are losers in poker. The less they know, the less they will bet into you, and the less they will try to bluff you. This means fewer decisions for you, fewer chances to guess wrong. Meanwhile, they're just trying to figure you out while you take the play to them. Never check-raising is an open invitation to other players to try to run over you every time you check, because they will know your check means you have nothing.

Johnny Quads' Corner

Some misguided players think check-raising is some-how wrong because it is deceptive and such a cruel body blow to an unsuspecting foe. They are wrong. It is deceptive, yes, and that is why it is right.

Even a move as simple as checking the nut straight you hit on the river sends a message. You gain an extra bet when the person who's been betting with top pair/top kicker the whole hand bets into you again after you check, and you then check-raise to win an extra-big bet. But you gain more than that. Next time, she won't be so quick to bet.

You must evaluate whether the check-raise or straight play will maximize your profit before you act. If your check-raise makes it one more bet to most of the table, they will usu-ally call. If it makes it two bets to go, they will usually fold.

Texas Truths

Check-raise bluffs are very rare in poker, especially at lower limits. If someone check-raises, that's usually your cue to run for the hills, and if you have check-raised an expert player hoping to win that extra bet, it could backfire, because she might dump her hand faster than you can say "dead giveaway."

Monster Hands

Despite the element of risk in giving free cards, there are a few times when checking is more profitable than betting.

- You flopped a hand with "all the cards," like an ace-high flush, four of a kind, or full house. Check and let them catch up.
- You flopped top set and a bet will fold everyone. Let someone else do the betting; check-raise on the turn or river.
- You have the nuts on the river and you're sure a check will induce a bluff, but a bet will fold everyone.
- You are sure you have a better hand than your aggressive opponent, and you are certain he will bet if you check. Check-raise.
- You have a hand so good another card can't hurt you. Take a chance on giving a free card.
- You know your opponents will fold if you bet, but the odds of them catching you are slim.

And if you find aces or kings on the button and everyone has folded to you, take a chance and let the blinds in free, if it won't look suspicious.

Big-Pair Deception

Big pocket pairs are your dream hands, so you want to win big when you get them. After all, the chance of getting aces or kings is 110-to-1. In a loose game with lots of folks seeing the flop, you should bet and raise and thin the field as much as you can. Don't worry, you'll have callers. But in a tight game against a bunch of Vegas rocks, you must be more subtle (unless you're the table maniac). You don't want everyone to fold preflop. You'll let a few players limp in and take the small risk of a crazy flop. You'll hope someone hits a top pair, like queens or jacks, while you have aces or kings.

Johnny Quads' Corner

Some of your tablemates will never slow-play a high pocket pair. Others will frequently. Noticing a pattern here is a major clue to discovering who is deceptive and who is not. You should keep a mental list of the devious players.

Slow-play isn't a move you use all the time. Tricky plays should be the exception, not the rule, in low-and middle-limit Hold'em. They play a greater role in high-limit and tournament play. Trapping is a part of your arsenal that you bring out when necessary, depending on the game and situation. What's important is that you have sent a message, and others know that even when you appear weak, the weakness could hide strength. It could hide just about anything—like pocket aces or a mortal lock.

Chapter 6
Starting Hands: The Critical Decision

Hold'em is crammed with subtleties that can cost you big money, and the best way to avoid the wallet-busting whirlpool is to make your initial decision—whether to enter the hand in the first place—a sound one. Your hole cards aren't glued to your fingers; they are easy to toss into the muck pile. Like the first small trickle from a failing dike, playing the wrong starting cards leads to a disastrous flood of chips from your stack into the waiting arms of the enemy.

The Power of High Cards

In limit Hold'em (where you will spend most of your Hold'em life, unless you are exclusively a tournament player), you don't make money with one tricky trap or bad beat, and you won't lose it that way either. You make money by playing better hands than your foes and getting full value from your holding, just like you pump out an oil well until it's dry. High cards beat low cards, and this simplistic-sounding principle is the beginning of sound starting-hand strategy. You play high cards, and you get the most out of them, usually by betting and raising strongly.

You can't be shy about betting in this game, as you discovered in the last chapter on isolation. Many of your power hands do not play well against a lot of opponents, so aggressive play is essential. Unless you are practicing slow-playing, which is the exception, you need to bet it up with the good hands and fold the bad ones. You also don't want to be a table maniac betting it up with all sorts of borderline hands, or pretty soon players will welcome your bets and beat you into the pot with their calls. Your bets will have lost respect, and you will be unable to protect your good hands from the onslaught of the masses.

Texas Truths

Hold'em has 1,326 possible starting hands. Because of the four suits, there are six ways of making a pair, and sixteen ways of making any other hand. Offsuit hands (8♠-6♥) are the same, so there are actually only 169 distinctly different hands: 78 suited hands, 78 unsuited hands, and 13 pairs.

Dominated Hands

High pocket pairs (A-A, K-K, Q-Q) and high cards with high kickers (like A-K) are where the power is. Since it is 16-to-1 against being dealt a pocket pair, many more of your playable hands will be of the A-K, A-Q, A-J, K-Q, or K-J variety. The higher the cards are, the less chance there is of the dreaded overcard. With A-K, if you pair either hole card on the flop, as you will almost a third of the time, you will own the top pair with the top kicker. This is what you seek in Hold'em in its most elemental form. You get the top pair and the top kicker, and you drive it home.

If you have A-K with a flop like K♥-8♥-5♣, you don't have to worry about someone with some crazy two pair or straight draw, because your aggressive preflop raise will have folded hands like K-8, K-5, 7-6, and 8-5. If someone has a heart-draw with A♥-10♥, well, you'll have to live with that. Make him pay.

What you hope for with your high-card or high-kicker power hand is that someone will play K-8, or ace-rag; these are dominated hands and are huge money losers. Sure, she'll hit two pair 2 percent of the time, but the rest of the time she'll pay you off with her king or ace and a losing kicker.

If you have a card in common and your opponent starts with a kicker lower than yours, as in A-K versus A-9, he must pair his kicker to beat you (barring some freak board like 8-7-6-5-2). He has just three outs. If he doesn't strike gold on the flop, he's just 12 percent to hit a nine by the river. If an ace hits—what he dreamed of when he first spied his hole cards—he is trapped like a rat. His A-9 is no better than an A-2 if you have a higher kicker. He still has to pair his off-card.

If neither of you pairs up, you still have him beat. Against a small field, the power hands can often take the pot with no improvement.

Johnny Quads' Corner

You can lose a lot of chips with second-best hands, and that's what high cards with poor kickers turn out to be. They start second, and they finish second. Folding would have been a cheaper option.

Pair Versus Pair

The other domination nightmare is pair over pair. You are about an 80 percent favorite if you have a pocket pair fighting a lower pocket pair. If you have aces, it doesn't matter if your foe has kings or deuces; she still has to make a set to beat you. This is a cruel scenario and you do not want to find yourself on the sucker end of it, so be extra careful with lower pocket pairs.

Punishing dominated hands, and avoiding them, is the genesis of good starting-hand play. You want to play good cards, and go in raising.

Odds of Being Dealt Hold'em Starting Hands

Any pair	16-1	6%
Aces	220-1	.5%
Kings	220-1	.5%
Aces or kings	110-1	.9%
Aces/kings/queens	73-1	1.4%
A-K (any)	82-1	1.2%
A-K suited	331-1	.3%
Suited connectors	27-1	4%
1 or more aces	6-1	15%
A pair or an ace	4-1	20%
2 suited cards	3-1	24%
Unsuited connectors	7.5-1	12%
A top-10 hand	22-1	4.5%
A top-20 hand	9-1	9.5%

Which Hands Are Winners?

Except for a pair of aces, any preflop hand can be folded. The value of starting hands varies according to several factors you must consider before committing a cent to the pot:

1. Position! Are you in the blinds, early, middle, or late?
2. Type of game: No-fold'em or tight as a drum?
3. Number of players who have already called.
4. Number of players you believe will call after you.
5. Any raises so far? Any expected after you?
6. The type of players in the game: novice, pro, and so on.
7. Are the players already in the hand tight or loose?

Guidelines for Starting Hands

Every Hold'em book has its own starting-hand criteria. No two are exactly alike, just as no two players attack the game in exactly the same way. That is part of its beauty and challenge. They all stress high cards, of course. Most books also detail how position affects the hands that can be played early, middle, and late, because you do not know the size of the field and if anyone will raise if you are among the first to act. Many philosophies go wrong, however, in failing to stress the importance of whether a game is loose or tight in deciding which hands are playable.

 Johnny Quads' Corner

Take the "raise" test. Look at your early-position hand. If a raise will make you sweat, it's not good enough. If you have to think long and hard about whether to call a raise with it, the hand is not playable.

Take early-position recommendations. You should always play the premium hands: aces, kings, queens, any A-K, and any A-Q. If the game is an aggressive one with tight, solid players for serious money, this might be as far as you can go. You play very few hands, but you raise with the ones you do play (not just aces). There is just too much chance of a raise and reraise after you, and the field will be small.

In an average game, you can add jacks, tens, A-J suited, and K-Q suited. These latter hands, however, are difficult to call high-stakes raises with against expert players because they are too easily dominated by likely raising hands. If there is little raising occurring, you could add A-J, K-Q, A-10 suited and even nines and eights, but you might limp in with these. You may add these hands as well if the game is aggressive, but the raisers are loose maniacs playing borderline cards. And if you're embroiled in a low-stakes limp-fest where almost everyone limps in preflop and there is rarely a raise, you can even play your drawing hands: high and medium suited connectors (Q-J down to 7-6) and all the pairs—without raising, of course.

Playing early position is a matter of survival. You use patience and discipline to tiptoe through this minefield until you get to the moneymaking later streets.

Middle Position

Your killer hands (A-A, K-K, Q-Q, A-K) are just as strong in middle position as early. If no one has raised, you raise. If there is a raise, then reraise. With A-Q, A-J, A-10, and K-Q, you always raise if no one has raised. If there is an early-position raise in front of you, consider just calling. If it's from the world's tightest player, you might even fold. If it's from a maniac, reraise. As you can see, your knowledge of your foes comes into play right from the start. (Always have that mental list of player profiles handy.)

Pairs such as jacks, tens, nines, and eights can cause problems. You need a small field to cut down on the overcards. If you think you can thin the field, raise like mad. If not, just call and then if overcards hit and you don't flop a set, they're probably headed for the muck. You should strongly consider folding preflop with all but the top four premium hands if it's already two raises to you in a tight game.

 Texas Truths

> If you're the aggressor preflop and no one has slowed you down, go ahead and bet on the flop. Your opponents have probably not made anything, and a bet could win you the pot right there.

Some borderline hands come into play in middle position: any suited ace, K-J, Q-J, J-10, and suited connectors down to 7-6. If you're first in, take control by raising. If there are limpers in front of you and it's a passive game, you can raise or limp in. If there's one raise to you, dump the hands in a tight game but just call in a loose game if late raises are rare.

In general, players with these hands don't want to call raises. Unless you are taking control of a small field or in a passive game, these hands cry out for a large number of passive players to pay them off if they hit a straight or flush. Suited aces and suited connectors are drawing hands that are not looking to pair a hold card, because top pair with the connectors is not big enough and the aces have kicker trouble. In a passive game where almost everyone calls preflop, you can play all these drawing hands, but raising is futile. Get in cheap with your fingers crossed.

Late Position

In late position, you play all the hands from early and middle positions, as well as unsuited connectors down to 7-6 if there hasn't been a raise. Raise with all the early- and middle-position hands except the drawing hands (A-*x* suited where *x* is below ten and suited connectors) if there hasn't been a raise. Use your knowledge of the players and size of the field to decide which hands on the list to call a raise with. Unless it's a superloose game, don't call two or three raises with anything but the top premium hands. Raise with aces, kings, queens, and A-Ks even if there are raises to you. If you're first in the pot, raise with anything to buy the blinds. This "late steal" is expected and you must do it 80 or 90 percent of the time. If you only do it with your good hands, those hands will never be called.

 Johnny Quads' Corner

> If you play against the same crowd a lot, vary the way you play your starting hands and throw them a curve or two to keep them from getting a good read on you. Keep them guessing!

You must decide early what kind of hand you hold and what you plan to do with it. Is it a drawing hand or a power hand? Does it want a large field or a small one? Since you're in late position, you know pretty much what you'll be facing. Use this information to decide if you should call, raise, or fold. Don't enter the pot without a plan. Late position offers you the luxury of formulating an accurate, effective strategy.

Who Knows Position?

Notice who uses position strategy with their starting hands at your table, and who just plays the same hands in any position. Knowing who the "book players" are is a huge help when putting players on hands and evaluating their play.

If you pay attention, whether you're in the hand or just watching, you can identify some keys to opponents' play that will allow you to predict their cards like a world-class psychic! Observe a player, then ask yourself which start hands this person will call with, and which hands she'll raise with. Is she on the passive side or more aggressive? Will she defend her blind? After the flop, is she straightforward, or will she bluff, slow-play a winner, check-raise, or bet on a draw? Can you force her to fold on the flop, or will she call you all the way down with an average holding?

Probabilities of Starting Hands on the Flop

Pairing at least one hole card	32%
Pairing both hole cards	2%
Four-flush when suited	11%
Four-flush when not suited	2%
Flush with two suited cards	1%
Straight-flush draw with suited connectors	3.4%
Making a set with your pocket pair	12%
Making a full house with a pocket pair	1%
Trips with no pocket pair	1.3%
Straight draw with connectors	26%
A pair on the board	17%

Note: There are 19,600 ways to flop three cards when your hole cards are taken out of the deck.

Starting-Hand Strategies

A peek at the previous chart should tell you in no uncertain terms how unforgiving the flop can be. You're usually going to miss and have nothing more than you started with. This is why you take control preflop: to convince others you already have a formidable hand even without those three cards. This is also why you want to start with high cards. Pairing a hole card is the most likely outcome. High cards can make top pair on the flop (good!), but low cards make second or third pair (not good!).

 Texas Truths

> The odds of making a straight flush on the flop with suited connectors are 5,000-to-1. The odds of making quads with your pocket pair are 407-1.

Playing Aces, Kings, and Queens

You want a few callers with the three best hands in Hold'em; you just don't want a huge number of players against you. You want to win more than just the blinds, but you don't want five or more foes if you can help it. Unless your bets and raises will force *everyone* out, bet it up big. Bullets and cowboys are the only two start hands you ever slow-play. Never slow-play or get cute with queens.

Pocket Jacks, Tens, Nines, Eights

Because at least one overcard will flop more than half the time, these hands play the same. Bet big preflop to get the hand heads-up, where you have a fighting chance.

Make people have to call two or three bets cold (unless someone has raised who only plays high pocket pairs). If you're in control of the hand preflop, bet it strong on the flop, no matter what hits. If that bet is raised (especially if there is a scary board like A-K-J), muck the hand.

Pocket Sevens Through Deuces

Unless you are in a very tight, passive game where you can force most people to fold preflop and then buy the pot on the flop, these are drawing hands looking to flop a set into a large field. You're 7.5-1 against flopping that set, so get in cheaply. Limp in; don't call raises. In no-fold'em games, you will play eights, nines, tens, and even jacks this way. Without a set, the hands are going to lose money. With a set, you will rake in a nice pot.

 Johnny Quads' Corner

Don't fear the straight. If an ace hits the board on the flop and the board has not paired, there will *always* be a straight draw if a player is holding the correct two cards. You can't spend your Hold'em life worrying about a straight beating you.

Big Slick

Ace-king, also known as "big slick," is a monster hand, and even though rocks insist it is a drawing hand, you must play it strongly. Only pocket rockets and kinds can dominate you, so unless you sense (by knowing your rivals) that you face one of those hands, raise and reraise. You're a coin-flip against any lower pair, and you totally dominate all hands that are two unpaired cards—your most likely adversary. You play A-K for its high-card value against a small field, but A-K suited is also the 500-pound gorilla of drawing hands: it has overcards as well as nut flush and nut straight draws.

Ace-Queen

You should have no fear with A-Q (nicknamed "little slick") unless someone who only bets with A-A (American Airlines), kings, or big slick is raising strongly. Bet it big. Your biggest concern is big slick, a hand that would dominate you. It's 82-to-1 against your facing this hand, but you must keep both eyes open if you face strong action.

Ace-Jack, Ace-Ten, and King-Queen

These are bettable hands if you're first to raise the pot, otherwise you can only call with them. Against two raises, you dump them. It is very likely they are dominated, since most raising hands have you beat. Dominated ace-high hands are some of the biggest money drainers, although you can always play these hands with a large field if they are suited. When the stakes get high, with these hands you must ask yourself: is the raiser a wild man betting on a prayer, or a tight player who only bets with a big hand?

Don't think that hands like A-10 and A-J have great value for making a straight. Any straight draw containing an ace will always be an inside straight draw, a 17 percent chance with two cards to come, 9 percent on the river. With K-Q, any straight draw will be a gutshot unless J-10 flops.

Ace-Nine to Ace-Two Suited

These are great drawing hands and play well with a large field. You can even call raises with them if you are sure everyone else will as well. Since your ace is probably dominated, you are playing these hands strictly for their drawing value. You are seeking a four-flush, trips, two pair, or a miracle on the flop. You'll hit one of these scenarios about 16 percent of the time, but throw away the hand if you don't, unless you have pot odds to chase a longshot. Make sure that longshot is a winning hand, not second best.

Ace-Nine to Ace-Two Unsuited

These hands are borderline at best, and you should not call raises with them. They are worth a raise in middle or late position if you are first in the pot, and of course, you can always raise with them to steal the blinds. If you're the aggressive type and there's only a limper or two in front of you and you are on the button, you can raise to fold the blinds and then try to take the pot down on the flop. You can limp with them in a no-fold'em game. In general, though, these are trap hands.

 Johnny Quads' Corner

Beware of playing hands that are the top and bottom end of a straight, especially a high straight such as K-9. If Q-J-10 is on board, you have a king-high straight, but someone with ace-king has you beat.

Suited Kings

King-9 to K-2 suited should only be played in middle or late position in a passive game where almost everyone limps in preflop. Don't call raises with them. The hand is played to flop a flush draw (11 percent chance) or two pair (2 percent chance). If you just flop a pair of kings, you are almost certainly out-kicked. (Out-kicked means you have a kicker (off-card) lower than your opponent. This lower card means your hand is dominated and you are a heavy underdog.)

High Hands with No Ace

These hands are K-J and Q-J, suited or unsuited. Their play depends on the type of game you are in. In a standard or tight game, you fold them early and anytime there is a raise to you. If you are in middle or late position, you can raise if you are first in the pot. You can limp late if no one has raised, and you can always try to steal blinds with these hands. In a passive game where everyone folds, you can try to steamroll the table with these hands if there is no raise to you. In a no-fold'em game, these hands are much stronger suited and you play them for their drawing value, not their high cards; in this type of contest, you can add K-10, Q-10, and J-9. With hands in this group, suited is much stronger than unsuited.

Other Drawing Hands

These hands are J-10, suited or unsuited, and suited connectors 10-9, 9-8, 8-7, and 7-6. Jack-10 suited is a favorite drawing hand of many players not just because of the flush, but because it has the potential to make so many nut straights. It has two rather high cards as well, although they are easily dominated. Make no mistake this is a drawing hand, so unless the game is weak-passive and you can buy pots, play it like the other hands in this group—a strict drawing hand. You don't call raises, you dump them early, and you limp in cheaply. Again, if everyone in this game limps in and gambles, then you should have the odds to even call raises here. These holdings have the potential to win some big pots when they hit.

Texas Truths

As the game becomes looser and more passive, the value of suited starting hands and connectors increases, and the value of power hands such as A-K and Q-Q diminishes.

Unsuited Connectors

Unsuited connectors 10-9, 9-8, 8-7, and "one-gap" suited hands such as 10-8 and 9-7 should rarely be played, unless you can limp in late or on the blinds into a large field. Connectors have an advantage because they can make an open-end straight with three sets of cards. If you have 10-9, then Q-J, J-8, and 8-7 give you an open-end draw, and an open-ender is what you are hoping for. With one-gap hands like 9-7, however, only 10-8 or 8-6 on the board will provide a good draw. An advantage of one-gappers is that they have an element of surprise and the straight is usually the nuts, but making a flush with these hands may cost you money. Connectors are also dangerous. If you play 9-8 and Q-J-10 is on the board, you have the "ignorant" (low) end of the straight. Someone with a real hand, A-K, can easily beat you.

Trash Hands

All other hands are money-losing trash that should be played only in the small blind into a large group for that last half bet, or if you like to gamble in the big blind for one raise into a huge, passive field. And it doesn't matter if your loser hand is suited. You'll only flop a four-flush once every nine hands. You'll make a flush only about 6 percent of the time, and a third of those will be runner-runner! If you're praying for a miracle flop for your 8-2 suited (pairing both hole cards, trips, flush, straight, full house, four of a kind), that fortunate happenstance will occur just once every twenty-one tries. Still, it's the miracle you hope for; you won't win by pairing a hole card.

 Shark Bites

Watch out for books giving you a strict list of playable hands: "Starting hands actually move up and down the hand rankings depending on the circumstance. Because of this, it can be a mistake to rigidly adhere to the hand rankings."
—David Sklansky and Mason Malmuth, *Hold'em Poker for Advanced Players*

In computer simulations, A-K suited will win in a four-player field about 44 percent of the time when all play to the river, while 8-2 suited will bring home the bacon just 19 percent of the time. With ten players, the percentages are 24 and 8. In actual practice, though, the advantage for the power hands is much greater, because they can bet and take control and win even when everyone flops "nothing," which is the usual state of affairs.

Preflop control is a huge psychological edge. If the 8-2 pairs a hole card, it is of no help unless the game is heads-up, because there's an 87 percent chance of an overcard. There will be two or more overcards 47 percent of the time. It is very difficult to bet into this power. If the flop is K-Q-8 or A-8-7 and someone raises preflop and now bets into you, do you really want to call bets all the way to the river with your pair of eights and deuce kicker?

Sometimes you'll find yourself in a game where everyone is playing trash hands—and winning with them. Before you are tempted to play garbage, remember that just because a trash hand is taking almost every pot, that doesn't mean your trash hand will win it.

Playing the Blinds

I've alluded to an aggressive blind strategy. In the blinds, aggressive means just seeing lots of flops but not aggressively raising, which you do only with premium hands or if you sense serious weakness. Remember, you will be at a positional disadvantage on all future streets. You can limp in with trash in a loose-passive game, and that's about it. Field size and raises are the determining factors here, because you are gambling a bit. In higher-stakes games, you won't try this as often, but if someone keeps stealing your blind from late position, you'll have to take a stand and play back at him sooner rather than later. Try to do it heads-up. If the game is short-handed (three to six players), the blinds come around awfully quickly and can eat you up, so play more hands and defend your blinds more aggressively. When it's heads-up, which is poker's equivalent of psychological warfare, you will usually defend your blind and often raise. Heads-up has some similarities to no-limit in that it's more about aggression and betting and less about the cards.

 Johnny Quads' Corner

Pay attention to which players defend their big blind with any hand and which defend only with reasonable cards. You can pick up some easy money this way, as well as find a key to an adversary's overall playing style.

In an average or tight game where you face small fields and premium hands, don't put a half bet in the small blind if it wouldn't have been worth a full bet, and in the big blind be wary of trap hands. If you call a single raise in the big blind with Q-6 offsuit and a queen flops, what do you do? Your six kicker is worthless. If you bet and are raised, you're finished. If you don't bet, someone will bet into you. Then what? You're out of position with a bad kicker. You want cheap miracles in the blind, or nothing at all.

If you're facing one or both blinds and the flop comes ragged, watch out if you let the blinds in without a raise.

They could have anything. A lousy flop like 8-6-3 is right up the big blind's alley with his mediocre, random hand. If he bets, you could easily be looking at two pair. Make the blinds fold!

Now, let's look at the flop.

Chapter 7
The Flop: Hold'em's Moment of Truth

The exposure of the three flop cards is the crucial moment in Hold'em. You now have five cards—a real poker hand—but you still have mountains to climb, and the path is fraught with peril. The flop is where poor players lose their way (and their money) and where good players reach the pinnacle of greatness. If you master the flop, the troublesome part of your journey will be behind you, and the rest of the road will be paved with gold.

A Time to Bet, a Time to Fold

The flop is the street of decision, the critical juncture. You must somehow quickly integrate three fresh cards into your hand—and your head. There are only two cards to come, and if you pursue them, you will pay dearly for each of them one at a time. You're standing at the crossroads, but no one is pushing you into the street. If your hand hasn't panned out, you can throw it away and live to fight another day. Folding on the flop is a fine art not an act of cowardice.

 Texas Truths

> Discretion is often the better part of valor in Hold'em, and only a fool clings to cards that are beat, no matter how beautiful they looked before the flop.

Think of your hole cards as your new bar squeeze at closing time. The flop will sober you up quickly, and suddenly the squeeze can appear a lot different. Other times your hole cards will stay true and faithful, but it's still a long way to that mountaintop where the pot of gold awaits. If you're still in there swinging, you want to be aggressive. The flop is no place for the faint of heart.

When those three cards hit, there are multiple calculations to make. Be sure you make them with the calm, inscrutable, steely-eyed grace of a poker champion. Don't stare at the board, screw up your face, and check your hole cards while your eyes dart back forth between your hand and the flop. You should have your hole cards memorized, and your reaction should be the same whether the flop made you or killed you.

Johnny Quads' Corner

If you are playing limits that are too low, buying the pot on the flop with nothing and thinning the field becomes difficult. Your poker moves are predicated on your bets having some bite. Play at a limit high enough to make your adversaries squirm.

Did the Flop Help You?

With a great hand like A-Q suited, if you pair a hole card, it will likely be top pair with top kicker, so you will have a very strong hand almost a third of the time. If you count two pair, trips, miracle flops, and straight and flush draws, a hand like this will flop something 52 percent of the time! Since you raised and reraised preflop, you will definitely bet with any of these hands, even the draws. In fact, if other players just called your raise, you have control. With many flops, you will bet whether you hit something or not, representing a high pocket pair, and try to buy the pot.

However, if you just limped in preflop with a borderline hand such as unsuited connectors (9-8), then unless you have hit a flop with 7-6, 10-7, or J-10 for an open-end straight draw (or a ridiculous longshot flop like Q-8-8), you check and fold.

Did the Flop Help Others?

This is when your knowledge of the individual players is the difference between winning and losing. Remember the preflop betting, calling, and raising pattern and, especially, who the preflop raiser was (if not you). Some players only play certain hands in certain positions. They will limp with some hands, call a raise with others, and raise and reraise with still others. Who's loose or tight, a novice or an experienced player? This knowledge is essential to putting players on hands postflop.

If you raised with 10-10, and the flop is 8♠-6♠-5♥, and someone bets into you, who would play any of these cards for a raise? Would anyone play 9-7 or 7-4? Are the blinds still in? If so, would they call a preflop raise with 8-6, 8-5, or 6-5? Is your opponent an aggressive type who will bet on a flush draw or any pair with a ragged flop like this? Is the raiser experienced enough to put you on an ace-face hand and thus try to force you out even though the flop missed him as well?

On the other hand, if the flop is A-K-8 and there is betting, your tens are history. Or if you have A♠-K♠ and the flop is 10♣-9♣-8♣, these cards are too powerful and too much in the line of what people play for you to continue. Remember, if someone has a ten, nine, or eight in this scenario, you are more than a 3-1 underdog, and even if you make aces or kings, you still might get beaten by a flush.

As always, the size of the field is critical. The larger the field is, the greater the probability that someone has hit the flop. If you've gotten it heads-up preflop, you always have a fighting chance if you know your player.

This is why in high-limit and no-limit games, experts try hard to force people out preflop. It is rare in those games to have more than three players see a flop.

Odds That the Flop Contains:

Flop	Odds	Percent
A pair	5-1	17%
Three suited cards	18-1	5.2%
Three of a given suit	72-1	1.3%
Two suited cards	0.8-1	55%
Three different suits	1.5-1	40%
Three in sequence	28-1	3.5%
Two in sequence	5-1	40%
None in sequence	0.8-1	56%
Three of a kind	424-1	0.24%
Note: Odds given are odds against.		

Raising Provides Clues

If you stepped up and raised preflop, you will usually raise postflop as well—and so will your foes. The preflop raise makes money, thins the field, and yields information from the way others respond to the wager. In return for the payoff, however, you have put a bull's-eye on your chest. People will be watching you. They are putting you on certain hands, eliminating others. You must do the same when they raise. Let's hope they are more predictable than you are. Many players have strict guidelines on which hands they raise with preflop. Often, the older the player, the more conservative they get. Many won't even raise with A-K. You need to get a line on this quickly.

When the flop hits, compare it to the hand you put the preflop raiser on. Bet into him if you think he missed. If he comes out betting, watch his body language. Is the bet believable, or is something a little off? If you are on a draw-ing hand like J♥-10♥ or 6-6, you can quickly jettison your hand if you missed; a quick, easy fold is part of their value.

The Ol' Switcheroo

Because you are under a microscope when you raise, you must throw people a curve once in a while. You must vary your play, not just preflop, but on all streets. You can't be too predictable, especially since you'll miss the flop more often than not. You want to bet your power hands, but occasionally don't raise with A-A, maybe raise with 5-5 or 8-7s instead. You'll usually bump it up strong with A-K, but you also might check now and then. The more astute your opponents are, the more you can cross them up, because they are paying attention. Against poor players who look no farther than their own two cards, don't waste your time with any fancy moves or advanced strategy—they aren't watching you. Just play a straightforward power game and take their money by showing them a better hand. You will beat inferior players simply because they play second-best hands and stay with them too long.

Loose and Tight

Your evaluation of whether an opponent plays lots of hands or just a few and how he or she responds to raise pressure is crucial to good flop play. For example, some people will never play a card below six; others won't play one below ten. How does a flop fit with your opponents' styles? If the flop is Q-10-10, you might fear trip tens, but if it is Q-4-4, do you need to fear three fours? If a flop is 6-5-4, would your foes ever play 8-7 or 3-2 for a preflop raise? If it is 8-7-5, would your rivals ever play 9-6 or 6-4?

Remember, your bread-and-butter hand is a top pair with a top kicker, and you must bet it strongly. If you don't have it, you need to represent it if you are the preflop bettor, unless the flop is a total nightmare (such as A-K-Q when you hold J-J).

Johnny Quads' Corner

The nature of the flop, the preflop and postflop betting, and your adversaries' tendencies should give you a good idea of what you are up against; then act accordingly, rationally and unemotionally.

Retreat

Any preflop hand can be folded, no matter how pretty. The wrong flop can decimate any hand, even pocket rockets. While you can't fear aberrations like a flopped set or two pairs, a very common problem is someone with an overpair. If you have 6-6 and the flop is K-Q-8, you have an 8 percent shot of making a set by the river to beat the kings, queens, or eights someone has. If you have two overcards, such as A-K against a pocket pair, you will hit an ace or king only 24 percent of the time on the turn or river. With one overcard, your chance is down to 13 percent. With one hole card paired, you have a 20 percent shot of beating that higher pair by making trips or two pair.

As the following table illustrates, some drawing hands have a fighting probability. If you have a four-flush on the flop, you have nine outs and a 35 percent chance. The same holds if you have paired a hole card and have an inside straight draw. An open-end straight has eight outs for a 32 percent shot, about 2-1 odds.

Chances of Making a Hand after the Flop

Outs	2 cards to go	1 card to go	Comment
20	68%	44%	
19	65%	41%	
18	62%	39%	Open straight flush draw w/1 overcard
17	60%	37%	
16	57%	35%	
15	54%	33%	Straight-flush draw open-ended
14	51%	30%	Still better than 50-50
13	48%	28%	Open-ender w/a pair
12	45%	26%	Four-flush w/ winning overcard
11	42%	24%	Four-straight w/ winning overcard
10	38%	22%	Flopped set, no full house on turn
9	35%	20%	Four-flush on the flop
8	32%	17%	Four-straight, open-ended

7	28%	15%	Inside straight w/ winning overcard
6	24%	13%	Need to pair either hole card
5	20%	11%	Paired a hole card, need to hit kicker
4	17%	9%	Inside straight/both hole cards paired
3	13%	7%	Need to pair a specific hole card
2	8%	4%	Pocket pair, need a set
1	4%	2%	Need 1 specific card in the deck

Note: Percentages are rounded off. This chart should be second nature to all Hold'em players.

The Texture of Flops

With more than 19,000 possible three-card combinations, learning flop play might seem daunting, but it's not that bad. Flops fall into distinct patterns. The following is a rundown.

Three of a Kind on the Flop

Example: Q♠-Q♥-Q♦. You don't figure someone for the case queen, so pocket pairs are strong here. Bet any pocket pair strongly, maybe even ace-face.

High Pair/Lower Kicker

Example: K♠-K♥-8♦. Trips are not as probable as you might fear. Yes, people play kings, but there are only two of them left in the deck. Having an eight is strong and worth a bet into a small field.

High Kicker/Lower Pair

Example: A♠-5♥-5♣. If someone bets, an ace is much more probable than a five in the hole. Many players won't play a hand with even one low card unless it's a pocket pair or A-*x* suited, and then not for a raise.

Three to a Straight Flush

Example: J♥-10♥-9♥. With high cards and tons of straight and flush possibilities, a flop like this can send even the toughest players running for cover. A lower sequence like 6♥-5♥-4♥ isn't quite as frightening.

Three of a Suit

Example: Q♣-9♣-6♣. These are the flops all those loose players who play any two suited cards, such as 8♣-5♣, love to see. It keeps them playing that trash. Against a big field, someone may have the flush already. Against a smaller field, bet right out with your queen or nine as if the cards were unsuited. Having the ace or king of clubs is a playable hand here if no one's raising; sometimes it's even worth a bet into a weak field. You are a 2-1 shot to hit that fourth club by the river. However, if others are holding a high club also, then your chances diminish accordingly.

Three Cards in Sequence

Example: J♥-10♣-9♦. Someone certainly has a straight draw if the sequence is a high one; a made straight and two pair are also possible. You don't fear straights as much as flushes in Hold'em, but sequences are tailor-made for players who love connectors. With lower rows such as 7-6-5, you need to know your players to decide if someone would have played cards to connect with this board. A preflop raise would eliminate your worries here.

 Texas Truths

> The more players who see a flop, the greater the power of the drawing hands and the less the power of the high pairs.

Gap Flops

Example: J♣-10♥-8♠ and J♣-10♥-7♠. A player might have a straight draw, but she would need a nine for an open-ender in the first example, and in the second, the draw will always be to a gutshot. The lower the cards are, the less chance of someone having the straight. In the first example, a player needs Q-9 or 9-7 to have the straight, 9-8 in the second—two perfect cards. The lower the gap flop is, the less chance that you are facing a problem. Only the blinds (or a blind man) would play 6-4 to connect with a board of 7-5-3. Here's where an analysis of the preflop betting and your adversaries will steer you in the right direction.

Two Suited Cards

Example: K♦-10♦-8♠. Since two flush cards will flop 55 percent of the time, you cannot live your life in fear of flushes. If only one player against you is suited, you only need to fear a four-flush once every nine hands. Still, you must be aware of it. Flushes are big moneymakers in this game. Loose players love to play suited cards. If you are in the lead on the flop, you must bet strongly, flush draw or not. No free cards here. If you thinned the field preflop, you're probably safe, but in a no-fold'em game, there is usually a flush draw out there with a flop like this.

Two Straight Cards

Example: A♠-Q♥-7♣, J♠-10♥-3♦, or K♠-8♥-7♣. If you worry about straights in Hold'em, you'll never bet. Almost every flop contains some kind of straight draw. The higher the cards are, the scarier the flop is, more because of the high-pair value than the straight. If there's an ace, any straight draw will be a gutshot.

Card Questions

How do I play against the toughest player at the table?
Very carefully. Make sure of one thing: the first time you take him on, make sure you win. Have a real hand that you can bet aggressively and that you can reraise with if he raises you. Don't let him steamroll you!

Three High Cards

Example: A♠-Q♥-10♣ or A♠-K♥-10 ♣. This is a scary flop if you raised preflop with a pocket pair and didn't hit a set. If you sense fear or you took control before the flop, you are obligated to bet at this flop or give it up. If you don't have top pair here, it might be time to run, unless you got it heads-up. If someone bets into you, you're taking a risk calling without top pair. Your opponents love to play these cards, and they usually fit right into a preflop raiser's hand, so they are a minefield.

Two High Cards

Example: A♥-K♣-6♦. This is also scary—if the flop missed you. If you were the preflop aggressor, you are obligated to bet.

Single High Card

Example: such as A♠-7♥-5♣ or Q♣-6♥-4♠. If a high card hits, hope it hits you. The preflop raiser is in the driver's seat here. As with all the high-card flops, the number of players against you determines how much you have to fear. Against a small field, you can buy the pot if you're first to bet. If someone bets into you, unless you can put her on a straight steal, you'll have to give it up. Any decent pocket pair plays well into a small field with this flop.

 Texas Truths

> All flops that do not have three of a kind or a pair will
> have a possible straight draw except Q-7-2, K-8-3, K-8-2,
> and K-7-2.

Ragged Flop

Example: 8♣-6♥-2♠. This flop favors preflop aggressors, anyone with a pocket pair, and the blinds if someone has let them limp in. If you played A♥-8♥ or 9♣-8♣, do whatever you can to force folds and take the pot right now.

Flop Tactics and Strategy

You maximize profits and minimize losses with how you play on the flop. Whether to bet, check, call, raise, or fold will be determined not just by your cards but by the preflop betting, your position, the size of the field, and the nature of the players against you. All the flop scenarios you will face from all the combinations of your pocket cards, the flop, and the complicating factors could fill thousands of pages, and that doesn't take into account your table image. In general, if you are on a draw, you want to get in cheap, unless by being aggressive you think you can win the pot through sheer force, either now or on a later street. If you believe you own the best hand, with all the draws that are usually present in any Hold'em hand, bet it big and strong to force others to fold.

Here are some general guidelines. Take them with you when you hit the green felt and start developing a feel for the correct play.

You Flop Top Pair

If you have top pair with top kicker, like A-K with an ace or king on the board (or an overpair in the pocket), you will bet if you're first to act and raise if someone has bet before you. If your kicker is not so good, bet if no one has bet yet; if someone has bet before you, give some serious thought to what he is betting on. If he has a better kicker, you might as well give up the hand. Your pair, no matter what the kicker, increases in value with a small field. With a large field, no hand is safe. It's a crapshoot, and any random flop could hide two pair.

You Flop Middle Pair

If the flop is A-Q-10, and you have Q-J or Q-8, you have middle pair. Playing middle pair is tricky. If someone bets, you must be able to read whether she has that ace. The preflop betting and knowledge of your foes will guide you here.

Johnny Quads' Corner

Against one or two players, middle pair can be strong; it is very strong in a heads-up game. In a large field, though, it's not worth much unless it has a draw along with it (as with Q-J).

Middle pair is much better with a flop like 8-7-5. Perhaps no one played an eight. If betting will get some overcards out, go to it. With this flop, and with Q-J, you have nine outs and a 1 in 3 chance of winning. You will have the odds to play this hand. If you bet, you will know where you stand. That information will help you play the hand on the more costly streets, and it won't be wasted because you still have a good chance at the pot.

You Flop Bottom Pair

Unless you're playing heads-up or have only two opponents, bottom pair isn't worth much. If you sense weakness or if they have checked to you, try to take it down. In a typical game, however, don't try to ram through third pair very often. In a passive no-fold'em game, you often will have odds to draw for two pair or trips.

You Have a Dynamite Draw

If you find yourself with a straight-flush draw, open-end straight draw (high end), flush draw, flush draw with a pair, or straight draw with a pair (even a gutshot), you have some decisions to make. Even though you are an underdog to win this one, you stand to get a good payoff if you hit.

Texas Truths

In fact, with an open-ended straight-flush draw, you actually are *favored* to make your hand. You have fifteen outs and a 54 percent chance.

With a large field, you won't be bluffing or taking control, so get in as cheaply as possible. You prefer a big field with a draw, so don't do anything to thin it out, and the odds will definitely be there to call all the way to the river. On the other hand, if you're a 4-1 shot to make your hand on the turn, as with most of these draws, you are actually making a great play if you bet or raise and have five or more callers. This goes for betting after the turn as well (see "Betting Odds" in Chapter 4).

With a small field, you must weigh thinning the field even more against your chance of winning the pot by sheer force even if you don't complete your hand. Draws generally want a large field, but sometimes raising as if you have a made hand will win you the pot if you miss, as you will more often than not (see "The Power of the Semibluff," Chapter 10).

Runner-runner flushes (23-1), pocket pairs needing a set (two outs), needing to pair your ace (three outs), and gutshots without a pair (four outs) are generally not good draws. Drawing with just two overcards needs good pot odds; they're a 7-1 dog to hit the turn. And if you have A-K and the flop is Q-9-8, hitting a hole card could make someone else two pair.

You Flop a Monster

If you flop four of a kind, a full house, flush, straight, or a set, you likely have the hand won already, and your thoughts move quickly from elation to how to suck every last chip out of your tablemates. First, remain calm. Act and bet in the same manner as always. Now think: would it look suspicious if you bet with a flop of 6-2-2 or A-2-2 (when you limped in the blind with 2-2 or J-2)?

 Johnny Quads' Corner

Ask yourself: how am I viewed at the table? If your opponents expect you to always run at pots and bluff, don't disappoint them. If you rarely bet, then you might check.

What would your opponents expect you to do with your typical hand in your position? If you raised preflop with Q-J and the flop is Q-J-10 or Q-J-J, and you always bet postflop, then bet.

Keep your usual pattern and do whatever will keep players in. In many games, folks want to play and won't believe you when you bet, so just bet right out. In tighter games, give free cards as necessary, but be careful. If there are drawing hands on board, you will have to protect the hand. If you have Q♠-J♠ and the flop is Q♥-J♥-10♣, there is definitely a straight draw out there, and a flush draw too. The same goes for flopping a set. Two pair and a set are much more vulnerable than nut flushes and full houses. Whether you get cute depends on the chance of someone getting lucky and beating you, and how obvious the hand is. Flushes are obvious; straights are often more hidden.

You Flop Nothing

Hey, welcome to Hold'em. You have nothing. But it's more important what others have. Maybe they missed too. If you're the preflop aggressor, you might be able to pick up the pot with a bet. Pause and give others a chance to whine about the flop and pick up their cards, ready to toss them in the muck. Skilled players don't automatically give up.

Overall, however, flopping nothing gives you a chance to get away from a disappointing hand without getting embroiled in an expensive side trip to Loserville.

Now, we'll move on to the turn card and the river, those expensive and challenging streets where the money is.

Chapter 8
Master the Turn for Rivers of Gold

Some say the turn is tough to play. Bets are twice as expensive as on the flop, and on the river, you either have it or you don't. But you have a wealth of information that will make you money on the turn. You know four of your opponents' six cards, you own six of your seven final cards, and you know your pot odds. Making sound decisions on the turn and the river isn't as difficult as you think. The hard part is finding a place for all your chips.

Slowly I Turn

The turn shouldn't scare you. You've seen how the rest of the table acted with their hole cards; you've seen the nature of the flop, the flop bets and raises, and then the turn card and others' reaction to it. So much of turn play is about having a read on your rivals and knowing the odds, and you have enough information now not to be groping in the dark.

You also should have a pretty good read on whether you are beat and whether your draw is a good one, so you can fold in the first instance and call in the second. If you have control on the flop, unless the turn card is a killer— such as a third flush card with a large, weak field or a card that pairs the board—you should keep the pressure on.

Card Questions

What should I do if an overcard hits the turn?
Don't always fear the worst here. Bet strongly. If players are checking the turn, they usually mean what they say: we're weak.

You want to take control wherever you can in this game. If you sense that your opponents are on draws, go ahead and bet, even if you are also. If there are four cards to a straight out there and you have nothing but a flush draw, go ahead and bet. No one's going to raise you, and you would've called anyway. Maybe you'll pick up a pot. Just bear in mind that if someone calls with top pair or what he believes is the best hand on the turn, he'll probably call on the river too.

Turn Up the Heat

With the stakes doubled, the turn is when someone can really put the screws to you if you are playing second pair or chasing with a draw. So folding is always an option, but it is so much better to be the aggressor. Use every chance to hit your opponents on the turn. The turn is the time of maximum financial pressure, and many lower-limit players like to see the turn card for one small bet but then will give up rather than call that larger turn bet. If you are going to force players out, it will probably be now. Most players who call the turn will throw in that last bet on the river, unless they are on a stone draw and have missed.

 Johnny Quads' Corner

> Don't think that just because someone called your flop bet that they have a real hand.

Many players are loose with their flop bets but tighter on the turn. Don't be afraid to fire another shot on the turn to make them squirm, even if you just have a draw. Watching players react to your turn bet can reveal volumes about their hands.

If you have a good read on your opponents' holdings, you should know whether to fear a third flush card, third straight card, or third high card on the turn. On the other hand, if you've been the aggressor, a blank can only help you. A bet could pick up the pot.

Tips for the Turn

Here's a little food for thought as you approach the river:

- If you bet preflop and on the flop, and then check the turn, you will be giving away that you have A-K or A-Q.
- Unless there is a raise war on the turn, you should have pot odds to see the river if you had the odds to see the turn.
- If the board pairs on the turn, do you need to fear trips? Had you put someone on that pair on the flop? If you bet with top pair on the flop, did you think someone was calling with second or third pair, or a draw? The more opponents you have, the greater the chance that someone now has three of a kind.
- If there is a pair on board, your flush or straight draw is no longer to the nuts.

Down the River

The river is the street where your hopes are realized. It is also the boulevard of broken dreams. It is where you will take down that nice pot you have been building for yourself through skillful play. It is also where some "river rat" will steal it from you if her prayers are answered. If you were on a draw, the river will make or break you. If you hit, you usually will have no doubt you have won and can bet or check-raise with abandon. If you miss, you usually can't even call a single bet, because there isn't a hand out there you can beat. So you must dejectedly muck your losing cards, often handing a huge pot to your rival.

The following table tells you what to expect after all seven cards have been dealt. Because cards are shared in Hold'em, however, you can rule many holdings out during a given hand.

Chance of Making Hold'em Hands with Seven Cards

Hand	Probability
Royal Flush	0.003%
Straight Flush	0.03%
Four of a Kind	0.17%
Full House	2.6%
Flush	3%
Straight	4.6%
Three of a Kind	4.8%
Two Pair	23.5%
One Pair	44%
High Card	17.4%

Note: There are 133,784,560 possible seven-card hands. This chart shows the results you can expect if you played every hand to the river.

Identifying the Best Hand Possible

Good Hold'em players can look at the board and instantly know the best hand at any point in the hand, especially the all-important river. It is a necessary skill. Knowing the nuts is one of the advantages of the game. Here's a rundown:

If there are three or more cards to a straight flush on board, a straight flush is possible and would be the nuts, but a flush is much more probable. Don't fear straight flushes. If there are three or more unrelated cards of the same suit and no pair, a flush is the nuts.

If there is a pair on the board, four of a kind is the nuts, but a full house or trips are more likely. There is never a nut hand less than trips in Texas Hold'em.

If there is no pair and if three or more cards to a straight are on board, as in A-J-10-6-5, and three or more cards of the same suit are not present, a straight is the nuts (K-Q). This is a more probable straight than if the board is A-J-7-5-3, when a 6-4 is needed. Possible straights are very common in Hold'em, but they can usually be discounted unless players are allowed to see many free cards.

If there is no straight possibility, as with K-J-8-6-2, a set is the nuts, as with hole cards J-J or 6-6.

Easy Street?

In many ways, especially if you are adept at figuring out what your opponents are holding, the river is a simple street to play. You know the nut hand, and how your table-mates have played through all seven cards. Either you have made your draw, or you haven't. It was the nut draw, or it wasn't. Others have made their draws, or they haven't. You had the lead going into the river, or you didn't. The river helped you, or it didn't. You now must decide how to get maximum value from your hand on the river, and that will dictate whether you check, call, bet, or raise.

If You're Leading

Good river play is determined by your knowledge of your foes and your estimation of what cards they hold. Have you been the aggressor with the best hand? If you have, and a blank hits the river, of course you bet (unless a check will induce a bluff from an aggressive player). If you were betting aggressively on just a draw and a rag hits, go ahead and bet again. Maybe your rivals were on draws also.

But what if a scare card hits the board, like a third spade when two had appeared on the flop? Then you ask yourself if someone was playing her hand like a draw. If you have only one opponent, it's worth a bet if the flush is your only fear. With a large passive field, however, you have to believe someone was on a flush draw.

 Johnny Quads' Corner

Watch the reaction of the other players to the river card. Don't watch the board—watch them. You can look at the board later. Take your time and put opponents under the microscope.

Fear and Loathing

While a third flush card can be a red flag, straights are a little different. You don't always fear three cards to a straight, but four get your attention. Any time the river gives a fourth straight card ace through nine, you need to tread carefully. Say the board is A♣-Q♦-10♥-9♠, and you have A-10. You've been betting right along with a few callers, and then a jack hits the river. Now anyone with a king or eight has a straight. These are common cards people play, especially kings. They might not have called bets with just an eight for an inside straight draw, but they could easily be sticking around with A-8, Q-8, 10-8, or 9-8. You can't bet here.

However, if you've been betting with pocket jacks and the board is 8-6-4-2 rainbow and a five hits the river, chances are much less that someone is going to stick around with a seven or three to hit that inside straight. Now you bet for value and make players with a pair of eights pay you off.

Johnny Quads' Corner

If a turn-river pair hits (K-7-6-3-3), don't fear trips; but if you hold 7-6, anyone with a king or pocket pair higher than seven has your two pair beat. Be careful. Bet strongly on the flop with that low two pair to force folds.

The board pairing on the river definitely gives you a queasy feeling if you had a cinch best hand on the turn. If you have A♠-J♠ and the board is Q♠-10♠-8♦-6♠, and if a queen, ten, eight, or six pairs the board on the river, your flush is no longer the nuts. Someone could have been playing a set or two pair and has now filled up.

If you were ramming and jamming with top pair, as with A-K and a board of A-Q-J-9, someone may be calling you down with queens or jacks. A second queen or jack on the last card can be trouble.

Getting cute with straights can cost you. If you have Q-J and the flop is K-10-9 rainbow, you have flopped the nuts. You may decide to get greedy and slow-play it, but you'll wish you hadn't when a queen or jack hits the turn or river. Now anyone with the lone remaining straight card (a scenario that is quite likely) will split the pot with you. Worse, anyone holding A-Q (if a jack hit) or A-J (if a queen hit) now has you beat, and you will lose a lot of money.

A Time to Check

One of the scariest river cards is the fourth card of a suit, as in J♠-10♠-7♠-6♥-2♠. If you hold J♥-10♣ for two pair or Q♠-9♠ for a flopped flush, the deuce of spades absolutely kills you. You definitely must check here. Players love to call flops like this with an ace or king of the flush suit (A♠ or K♠). They know that if a fourth spade hits on the river, they win. If you flop a low flush like this, you must make the chasers pay.

What Not to Fear

While an ace or a high overcard will always get your attention, in general don't panic over possible hands made on both the turn and river. Most players don't hang around for runner-runner if there has been financial pressure. If the board is Q♠-10♠-8♥-7♥-4♥, don't fear the flush. If the river had been a spade, that's something else. And don't worry that a turn-river pair has made someone trips unless you put him on that pair after the turn, say with Q-

10-8-A-A and he bet. That's a lot different than Q-10-8-4-4. Now if you had K-Q, your two pair still wins over anyone holding a ten or eight or queen with a lower kicker.

A sequence that appears at the eleventh hour isn't scary, either, as in K-Q-7-6-5. Don't fear a straight here.

Betting the River

Bet for value on the river. Don't become timid and check just because there's a chance you might be beaten. If it's not probable that you are outmatched, go ahead and bet. If you win more than half the time with this play, do it. If an opponent has been in control of the hand, but you are going to call her on the river, bet if you're sure she won't raise. It won't cost you anymore and you might get her to lay down a better hand, especially if a scare card hit.

Don't bet with a borderline hand if the only players who will call you are ones who have you beat. Say you have A-Q and the board is a raggedy 10-8-7-5-2. You believe A-Q is good, but why bet? Anyone with a worse hand than yours will fold, and anyone with a pair will call you. It's a losing play.

 Shark Bites

"Conservative players are playing mostly good cards. If they bet . . . you just get out of their way."
—WSOP champion Dan Harrington

Don't "sheriff" the pot or call someone just to see his cards. If you don't believe you have a good shot at winning, don't bet. These losing bets add up and are hard to recoup. You should win most of the time on the river if you're betting or calling. If you aren't, you need to re-examine your game. If it's a decent-size pot, of course, and you have no read on your opponent, you may have to call to avoid a costly mistake. Small pots are easier to let go. But never toss in a bet on a prayer or because there is a remote chance someone is bluffing. That's what losers do.

Obviously, your decision is much different if someone has already called a bet or if there is a raise. No one's going to be bluffing here. Raise-bluffs and check-raise bluffs on the river are almost nonexistent in limit poker.

Calling River Bluffs

Many inexperienced players don't realize that a good bluff usually must be set up on the turn, rather than appearing out of thin air on the river. Watch for this, and if you have a tough call, look at your player. Is he on your tricky list? Or was his last bluff in the 1980s? Never bet that this is the one time a foe is bluffing.

If you're lost, you can use pot odds to help you. If the pot odds are greater than the chance he's bluffing, then call. For example, if the pot is $120 and the bet is $20, you're getting 6-1 odds. If he's a deceptive player who often tries to steal, the odds may be just 3-1 against him bluffing, so you call. Out of every four such situations, you will lose $20 three times for a $60 loss, but gain $120 when you catch him. That's a $60 profit.

However, if he is a straightforward player who is tight with a buck, maybe he'd attempt a bluff only once out of eleven such hands, so the odds would be 10-1 or more against him trying a steal. Catching him bluffing is a long-shot. So fold—6-to-1 on your money isn't enough.

Bluffing on the River

Stealing on the river is a play that won't always win for you, but it is one you'll have to make from time to time, if for no other reason than letting the other players know that you will do it. As you'll discover in the chapter on bluffing, good bluffs are set up on the turn, and they must be consistent with the way you have played the hand. They can't just come out of the blue.

Johnny Quads' Corner

Sometimes the only way to win a pot is with a stone-cold bluff on the river. It doesn't always succeed, but it doesn't have to work every time to be profitable.

However, if everyone checks to you, go ahead and bet. You only have to be successful occasionally to make this play lucrative. And if you have been the unchallenged aggressor in the hand, even if you now have nothing but a busted draw, you still must bet. The larger the field is, the greater the chance someone will call, but who knows, maybe they all missed as well. Here is where reading your fellow players is everything, and stealing this pot might be the difference between winning and losing this session.

Pummel Them

Bet into weakness. Give others a chance to show it, with their lack of betting and their mannerisms, their vibe. You can smell it in the air. A river bluff is often the only way you can win. Use it sparingly, but use it.

If the final card is a blank, sometimes being in early position can help you. If you're first to bet, this show of strength might take the pot. The same if a scare card, such as a third flush card or an ace, hits. If you're first in the pot, you might take it down if you previously played the hand as if it is plausible that you now have a flush, aces, or two pair—and no one else has made a real hand. You need decent-size stakes and a real feel for the game for this move.

Ask yourself: Is my adversary smart enough to lay down a hand, or will he just throw chips at the pot if I bluff? Are you viewed as Honest John or Tricky Dick?

In the next chapter, you will learn about the different species of human animals in the green-felt jungle, and how to conquer them.

Chapter 9
Loose, Tight, and Just Right

So many tough decisions in Hold'em come down to your knowledge of the players at the table. When you compete in a casino or a public cardroom, you are frequently sitting down with strangers. That's a huge disadvantage. Fortunately, most people use recognizable playing styles, whether they realize it or not, and it's not difficult to discover their overriding philosophy and strategies. That's an advantage, as long as you don't give your own style away.

Four Archetypal Playing Styles

There are four basic styles of play: loose-passive, tight-passive, loose-aggressive, and tight-aggressive. As noted in Chapter 1, "tight" means playing very few starting hands and folding quickly, while "loose" means playing many hands and seeing many streets with them. "Passive" denotes someone who calls lots of bets but rarely raises. "Aggressive" means someone who bets, raises, reraises, and bluffs often, and pushes every perceived advantage.

Your strategy against the four types will be markedly different. You may fit into one of these categories as well, but you will prevail because you will change your strategy based on the nature of the game you are in and the type of players at your table, and because you will disguise your type through misleading verbal and visual cues.

Loose-Passive

Loose-passive players, termed "calling stations," are the weak sisters of poker. Timid and predictable, they call your bets when you have a great hand and occasionally put a bad beat on you at the river with cards that leave you shaking your head. Most of the time, though, these players fatten your bankroll. They play too many starting hands and stay with them too long. They always seem to be second best at the showdown. They get to play a lot of hands, but they pay dearly for it. They win some pots, but that's just because they are in so many, and despite the pots they take down, they are often the big losers at the table.

Calling stations are epidemic in home games and no-fold'em games in many cardrooms, especially in

California. Whatever you do, don't discourage them from their chosen course. They are your meal ticket. If they put a bad beat on you, just say "nice hand," and mean it. Don't let them think for a moment that they played badly.

Johnny Quads' Corner

Calling stations are the most plentiful player type in friendly home games around the kitchen table.

These are "action players," but their action means just being in the hand, not betting it up. Folding a hand genuinely pains them. They believe in miracles and probably wear lucky underwear. They hit a two-outer a few weeks ago, so that keeps them coming back. They will call whether there are correct pot odds or not.

One of their failings is that, not only are they loose, but they are also passive. They don't put pressure on other players, so when they are in the lead, they don't force others out. It doesn't occur to them to use their passive image to steal pots. They just want to play. So, they get beat too often on those rare occasions when they flop top hand. And when they finally bet, astute players know to fold quickly, because the loose-passive must have a monster!

Forget trying to bluff out a calling station. They will call you on the river just to see your cards. They couldn't sleep at night if they didn't. You'll have to show these players a hand to win. The good news is you will usually have better starting cards. Calling stations are in love with any two suited cards and any two cards that look remotely like they might make a straight, so you'll see them playing 9-5 suited and 6-5 offsuit, regardless of position.

Tight-Passive

As mentioned in Chapter 1, tight-passives are derisively known as rocks and they play like their Social Security check is their stake. Sometimes called "weak-tight," these players will wait forever for a premium hand and then not bet it up. They are painfully frightened of bad beats and often enter hands fearfully. Apparently, they have had their aces and kings and ace-king cracked so often, that they won't ram and jam with them. Of course, you're going to get beat with them, dude, they're the only hands you play! No one wins every hand.

Rocks are either dour-faced whiners or grinders just trying to eke out one big bet per hour so they don't have to work at McDonald's. These players were like a virus in Vegas during the '90s when poker was dying. They're always harping on players or the dealer to "speed it up." They take no joy in the hand or even in winning a pot—it's their due. Usually older, they will tear into any young players who beat them with hands they "never should've played." You'll find them plopped down in low-limit day games in any casino.

Tight-passives are nothing if not predictable. If a rock bets, he has a hand, and he believes he has a right to the pot because of all his patient waiting. So, these players can be stubborn. They feel you should respect their tight image and give them the pot; as a result, bluffing them can be difficult. They play infrequently, so the best course is to get out of their way. That's what they want—a tiny pot with no risk. And the no-risk philosophy means they won't bluff, despite their image.

They hate it when you raise their blinds; so by all means, do so. These players are easily aggravated. If you like to have fun at others' expense and goof on cranky old cusses, keep up a steady stream of chatter. They'll soon be looking for another table.

 ## Shark Bites

> "Rocks think you should only win pots with the big cards
> . . . but they're wrong. You're supposed to win pots with
> any cards you can."
> —D. R. Sherer, *No Fold'em Hold'em*

Loose-Aggressive

Loose-aggressive players are much more fearsome than the previous two types, in fact, in some ways they are the scariest players at the table, though not the best. Still, beating them takes careful, patient, thoughtful play. Loose-aggressive "maniacs" are the wild men and women of Hold'em. They appear fearless and are always betting and raising, regardless of position. They raise and reraise so much that at first you think they must be the luckiest players in the world, or on a tremendous rush, until you realize that it is just their style to push any playable hand (and some unplayable ones) to the limit.

They are either gamblers looking to get lucky or average players taking advantage of others' willingness to fold.

Sometimes, maniacs are just players who read in a book somewhere that aggressive players win. They do take control and they do take down some pots—there's no question about that. Opponents know they will keep firing at the pot, and unless the limits are too low, they can win some chips through sheer force. They bet strongly on draws, adding an element of deception, and sometimes those draws hit.

Johnny Quads' Corner

Beware: The maniacs' hard-hitting style is perfect for a short-handed or heads-up game, in which you must play more hands and take control. You don't need premium holdings to take the pot short-handed, and waiting for top hands is a losing strategy. If you find yourself in a game that has suddenly grown to six players or fewer and there is a maniac present, leave the table.

Good players quickly catch on that the maniacs' aggression is not controlled and their betting is not calculated. After all, no one gets enough premium hands to justify that kind of constant aggression.

Superior players will patiently fold bad hands cheaply while waiting for good hands. They will use the maniacs' predictable raises to make more money when they get a top hand and pile onto the maniacs' aggressive play to thin the field when necessary or even isolate the loose-aggressive who usually will have a worse hand.

Maniacs love to gamble and can amass a big pile of chips in a hurry when they are hitting their draws, but that pile can dwindle to nothing just as quickly. Curiously, not always the expert players take down the maniac; sometimes it is the rocks and calling stations. The calling stations will call all the way to the river, often exposing the loose-aggressive's hand as nothing but bluster and dreams. The rock will wait patiently for a top hand that the maniac will be helpless against.

Maniacs lose because their aggression is not selective and they don't back off when they encounter strength. They seem unable to change gears when the table has figured them out. They only possess one speed—until their chips are gone. Without chips, they are nothing but a lot of hot air.

Tight-Aggressive

Tight-aggressive players are the experts of poker. They are assertive but not wild. They are selective about the starting hands they play. They bet strongly when they have a good hand or when they sense weakness but not on a prayer or just to take control if that control isn't going to win for them. These players can back off when they are no longer the favorite to win the hand. They have more than one speed and adapt to their fellow players and the game they are in. Experts play position. They use the tendencies and weaknesses of the other three types against them. Tight-aggressives don't just play their own cards; instead, they figure what the others have and use that knowledge to win or fold, gaining money in both situations.

Experts push every lead and advantage, are satisfied with safe, small pots, and usually enter a hand raising. They know when to back off, and they don't get rattled.

These players don't try to bluff players who aren't going to fold. They aren't constantly betting like the maniacs, so their bets maintain power and respect.

Experts pay attention and analyze their foes, unlike the other three types who often seem to play in a vacuum, oblivious to everything but their own cards and their rigid, immutable personal styles of play.

 Texas Truths

> If experts have a weakness, it is evident when they drop down from higher-limit games. In the habit of folding a lot of hands, they can be susceptible to a bluff and give players' holdings more credit than they deserve. Others play much too loose at the lower limits, in which case they surely lose.

Strategy Against the Four Types

As you might expect, strategy and tactics against the four types is markedly different. Your ability to adapt and, if need be, find a different game is what will make you a winner. Here are some tips:

- Only try to bluff the tight players, because the maniacs and calling stations are always going to be there at the river to pay you off. Rocks and experts will lay down a hand: rocks because they are cheap, experts because they are smart enough to fold.

- Isolate against the types most likely to be playing with weak cards: the maniacs and calling stations. If you can get them heads-up, you will usually be a big favorite.
- Never slow-play against loose players. Why would you want to? The calling station will call your bet, and the maniac might raise you! You might slow-play a rock if you want to risk the free card, but the expert might see through your ploy.
- The most likely bluffers are the maniac, who's usually semibluffing (bluffing with outs) half the time anyway, and the expert, who can smell weakness and will try to buy a pot at an opportune time. The rock is too tight to bluff, and the calling station doesn't have the stones.
- You want the players who will push the action (and cost you chips) sitting on your right: maniacs and experts. If an expert bets, you can fold cheaply. If a maniac bets, you can reraise and try to isolate her, thin the field, or make others pay off your superior hand. If these players were acting after you, you would be forced to fold hands that could not stand a raise.
- If there is a high-card flop, fear the rocks and experts. If the flop is ragged, it might have hit the loose players.
- If there are three suited cards on the board, be wary of the maniacs and calling stations. These loose players love to play any two suited cards and may have the flush.
- If there are three cards to a straight on board, such as 8-7-5, 9-8-6, 10-8-7, 6-5-4, and the like, don't be too quick to rule out a straight if you have maniacs and

calling stations in the hand. These loose players will see flops with hands 9-6, 6-4, 7-5, J-9, 9-6, and 8-7.

A general rule of thumb is: Against tight players, call less but bluff more. Against loose players, call more but bluff less. Paradoxically, in a very tight game, you can actually play more hands. Against a very loose table, you can also play a few more hands than usual.

 Shark Bites

As Bill "Bulldog" Sykes once wrote: "Rocks are tight with their money, but very free with their unsolicited advice."

One of the most profitable decisions you can make in your poker life is simply choosing the right table. Some games will just never be moneymakers. Listen for laughter—it means fun and probably some loose play. Why try to grind out a few bucks against a bunch of superserious, tightwad rocks? Tell the floorperson you want a different table.

The Game Is a "Type"

If you can classify the game you're in on a given night as loose-passive, loose-aggressive, tight-passive, or tight-aggressive, it is a major strategic breakthrough. Games usually have their own personality, and if you can tune into it, you can use this insight to beat it. Because of a poker peer pressure, people who play together often tend to play alike. In California, you might find 80 percent of the table loose, while in Vegas the ratio is reversed.

Good tip-offs are the number of players seeing the flop, how much raising and reraising is going on, and the types of hands being played. Game strategy and tactics are similar to structuring an attack on an individual player of that type.

The Loose-Passive Game

Against calling stations, you can see many more flops than usual because there are so many players in the pot and you can get in cheaply. You will not bluff much, but you will have odds to chase a lot of straights and flushes. You still will be one of the tighter players, and you will make money by quickly folding hands that do not materialize on the flop, while your foes will pay you off all the way to the river when you have a winner. This game can be quite profitable.

The Loose-Aggressive Game

Playing against maniacs can be problematic. If the game is filled with them, you have no choice but to hunker down or find a different game. You don't want to match them raise for raise on borderline holdings and hope to get lucky. That's what they do. You will need to wait for decent cards and isolate if possible. Rocks usually defeat the maniacs. If there are many players seeing the flop, try some drawing hands like A-*x* suited, but flops in this game don't come cheaply. You can try to isolate with your good hands, but this tactic doesn't always work against a group of maniacs looking to cap the betting preflop. You are going to have to be patient and endure some wild bank-roll swings here.

The good news is there are loads of chips being tossed around, so there is money to be made. You will be praying that you hit a draw or are dealt a monster before your chips run out. Since the game is loose, theoretically you can play more starting hands than normal, but with all the raising, you will need some discretion. Before every move, calculate how many players will be in the pot, how many raises you will have to call, and your odds.

The Tight-Passive Game

A tight-passive affair dominated by rocks can be a real snoozer. Their tight play allows you to push the action, but because they only play top hands, if you are called, you are usually facing a better hand. You can bluff if the flop is ragged, but be careful, rocks are stubborn. You can play looser than the field because they are so passive, but beware because rocks make their profits from loose players who play too many hands. This game is better left to older players who want to grind out a small hourly pittance. Go find a more interesting game.

Johnny Quads' Corner

If you are not more skilled than the other players at your table, you will have to get lucky to win.

The Tight-Aggressive Game

A game dominated by experts—good luck! How much do you want to pay for poker lessons? Playing a solid, positional, tight-aggressive style will give you a fighting chance, but you will have to catch some cards to show a profit. Meanwhile, the experts you are facing might have a few moves you haven't even heard of.

There's an old poker story of a guy who was the tenth-best Hold'em player in the world, but he always lost. Why? Because he played against the nine best players in the world.

Playing against a lot of experts is like beating your head against a wall. Why not just ask the floorperson for a table change?

That being said, if you have a few bad players in your game, even if there are many experts, you still could show a profit. Tread cautiously.

When They Bet

If a rock bets, of course you take notice. What woke him up? These players don't take chances, so a simple fold here is prudent.

If a calling station bets, figure she has the nuts because that behavior is so unusual. You must ask yourself: why is she betting for the first time in an hour?

If a maniac bets, well, when *doesn't* he bet? His wager doesn't mean much. He could have a hand, but more likely it's just a longshot draw. It's when he doesn't bet that you have to stop and think.

The expert, of course, is the player you have to watch. She's the one you need to worry about. A bet from her often means a hand, but it could also mean that she thinks you don't have one, or that she's sensed weakness and an opportunity.

First Impressions and Table Image

Average poker players never get past a new player's first impression when they evaluate his or her play, but you shouldn't be so simplistic. Pay attention to the hands a person shows down over time before jumping to conclusions about which style she plays. The amateur poker shrinks at your table will assume in all their wisdom that someone who looks unsure will play timidly (weak-tight), and a loud good ol' boy will be loose or a table bully. A guy with glasses and khaki pants will be pegged as a "thinker," someone who analyzes everything so overtly that he can be manipulated by fancy plays. Sure, personality helps in figuring someone out, but don't be hasty, and if you like to have fun, you can manipulate your table image to suit your own ends. You don't have to play like your personality or looks. In fact, you can play any way you want.

Texas Truths

If you can't decide between a conservative or wild image, choose wild. It's much more confusing and challenging for opponents.

If you're smart, you'll watch the table before you dive in. Take a close look: Who's an expert, and who's a novice? Who's a grinder, and who likes to bet it up? Who's tight, who's loose, and who's on tilt? Who's calmly in control? Who's ahead, and who's losing? Does the game have an overall personality? Decide which style will best beat this game. Then when you sit down, act in a manner *opposite* to how you intend to play.

For example, if the game is tight-passive, play a little looser and try to buy some pots when ragged flops miss your foes' A-K and A-Q. Act as though you don't have a ballsy bone in your body and would never dream of bluffing. Fold a whole bunch of starting hands when you first sit down, unless you get a monster like A-A, K-K, or A-K. If a queen flops, say, "Damn, I had pocket queens (or ace-queen)!" When the amazed rocks ask why you didn't play, just say, "I thought you had aces or kings!"

 Shark Bites

"A great poker player has to have really good instincts. He has to be able to feel out his opponent, try to outguess him, figure out what he's thinking. . . . I don't sit down at the table with a strategy. Sometimes it's right to be aggressive. Sometimes it's right to wait patiently. Whatever the players are doing, I react to it."
—tournament star Phil Ivey

A loose-passive game won't require much pretending. Everyone's calling no matter what you do. Act as though you came to gamble. See the flop for the first few hands.

Appear to play like one of the group, but in fact play a little tighter, and get away from trouble quickly on the flop.

In a loose-aggressive affair, act like one of the good-ol'-boy maniacs. Talk it up loudly, chat up the waitress, act as though you're half drunk, and be visible when you're betting and raising. Carelessly throw chips in the pot during your first several hands. Try to cover the fact you're playing fewer hands and are isolating, playing position, and betting with skill and cunning. Act as though your bets are just part of the wild party. If you win, act as if you got lucky.

If you're in a tight-aggressive contest with mostly solid players, your best bet is to leave. Your next-best strategy is to get respect and make them think you're a solid player. Act and talk as they do. Play tight-aggressive; don't play dumb. You want respect so they won't try to run you over, bluff you, or make you a target.

A Few to Watch For

Here are a few of the more-common cardroom denizens:

- **Grinders.** These lower-limit players are just trying to make an "hourly rate" of about one "big bet" ($10 in a $5–$10 game). They are impatient and often ornery; they push for fast play and take no real joy in winning a hand. They can wait forever for good cards to play—longer than you.
- **Tourists**. They're not on vacation to fold a lot of hands; they came to play. They are loose and will play some borderline hands. If they get lucky, good for them;

don't criticize how they play. They have a right to play however they want. Keep them happy.

- **Solid players.** Unlike grinders, they can be pleasant and have fun while they earn money. They are calm and in control and know when to be aggressive and when to play along, when to bluff and when it's futile. The really good ones can read you and your cards like a book.

- **Internet players.** These younger players have lost a lot of their "learning curve" money online. They aren't bad, but they aren't good either. They understand betting pretty well, but they don't understand people. They can't spot tells or hide their own. Stare at them for a while, and you'll find out what you need to know.

- **Twenty-something "kids."** They haven't been playing long enough to get it, and they are usually playing with money they can't afford to lose. This makes them play weak and too tight.

- **Dealers.** Many gambling houses let their employees sit in when they are off-duty. Although dealers spend hours running the game, most are average players at best. Don't fear them.

- **Macho types.** Controlling, loud, and blustery, they're too busy chatting up the cocktail server to concentrate on the game. They feel it is emasculating to fold, and their egos could never handle being bluffed out, so they will pay off your big hands.

- **Older women.** They've seen it all and probably learned the game when the "fair sex" was all but banned from poker. They play tight, but don't try to steamroll them; they've seen that move before.

When figuring out opponents, most players fail to ask the essential question: What motivates them? Why is this person here in this particular cardroom, right now, at this hour? Is she having fun, or is she serious about winning? Vacation or vocation? Is it competition, or a job? Desperation, or diversion? Why isn't he at home? Is he a regular here? One easy way of finding out is to make a little conversation.

Poker is more than just cards. Getting to know your tablemates can only help you.

Chapter 10
Betting, Bluffing, and Control

Betting is the language of poker; the more money behind your bet, the louder your voice. You send a message with your bets: you manipulate, coerce, pummel—even seduce. A bet can be a shadowy spy seeking information, a sledgehammer pounding your enemies into submission, or simply a way of maximizing profit on a given hand. A bet can also represent poker's most feared and devious art form: the stone-cold bluff.

Mr. Natural

Your courage, and all your poker skills—both mathematical and psychological—come together when you bet, just as a good golfer brings all his mental and physical skills together in a gorgeous arcing swing and solid contact with that elusive white ball. The golf swing is frighteningly complicated, but the pros just step up and hit it. They're not thinking about the hundreds of tips they've read in golf magazines and books. They're playing by feel. To clutter their minds with the myriad of golf instruction about their feet, grip, club angle, shaft direction, hip rotation, head position, knee flex, weight transfer, follow through, and so on would invite disaster.

Betting in poker is less physical but otherwise no different. Just as that same grooved golf swing, you should bet the same way every time. Push your bets out in a smooth, controlled, natural, consistent manner. If you must speak, always speak the same way, with the same inflection and tone. Look at one place when you bet, and don't push the chips out too fast or too slowly.

 Johnny Quads' Corner

Getting cute when you bet and trying fancy misleading moves (like betting in a timid manner when you are strong) usually backfires. Good players pick up on this stuff, and instead of deceiving people, you make yourself easier to read.

Also, if you are in a no-limit or pot-limit game or a game where the betting limits are not fixed, try to bet the same amount from hand to hand on the same streets. This consistency will prevent good players from getting a read on you through your bets, because you will appear the same, whether you have the nuts or are on a stone bluff.

If all these dos and don'ts on betting sound like so many golf tips, just remember that pros spent a lot of time on the practice tee before they got it right and could just "grip it and rip it." Practice betting the same way—by yourself and in lower-stakes games.

Effective Betting

Bets are used to take control of a hand by representing strength, forcing folds, sending a message, obtaining information, stealing a pot, or maximizing profit. This will never happen if foes do not respect your bets, because if you have a reputation as a maniac, chronic bluffer, or as someone who plays questionable cards, they will gleefully call or raise you.

For a bet to be effective, it must put opponents to a decision. Decisions often entail guesswork, and guessing means there is a chance of guessing wrong. That's money for you. If calling your bets is usually a good play for your adversaries, you're doing something wrong. Their decision is too easy.

You fight this through good solid play, but good play or not, it is essential that the money being wagered has some real value.

Texas Truths

The name *poker* comes from the French word "pocher," which means to bluff, and/or the German word "pochen," which means to boast. The element of bluff was the essence of the game from its inception. Poker is boring and inconsequential without something meaningful at risk.

If the stakes are too low, you cannot use your skills. It is just too easy for someone to call a bet. There is no pressure, no chance of a real mistake, no prospect of forcing a better hand to quit, and no opportunity to bluff or steal pots. You are not really playing poker. You're just tossing in money and seeing who gets lucky. Bets in poker must have some bite. There must be a squirm factor, or the game doesn't work. It ceases to be complex and becomes a showdown. How can you read a player who doesn't care about the money? This is a major reason you should avoid low-limit tables. Why hone that beautiful swing if others can score just by kicking the ball down the fairway?

The Comfort Zone

The easiest players to beat are those playing with "scared money." These players are in over their heads, playing limits that are too high or with money they cannot afford to lose. You want as many of these types at your table as possible; seek out these games. Players' reactions to the stakes matter, not the stakes themselves.

If you're playing with college kids using their food money as a stake, a $4–$8 game might be way over their heads. You can be very aggressive and bet them out of pots. Control, intimidate, and steal the money. Bluff away. Players who use scared money become timid. They won't bluff, chase draws, or play borderline hands or second pairs. They are reduced to waiting for a monster. You can pummel them hand after hand. If they wake up with the nuts, you cheaply fold. They're out of their comfort zone.

 Shark Bites

As poker legend Doyle Brunson writes in *Doyle Brunson's Super System:* "If I find somebody I can keep betting at and he keeps saying 'Take it, Doyle, take it, Doyle' . . . then I'm going to keep pounding on him. I'm not going to let up."

If there's a rich kid or dot-com moneybags in the game, the stakes might be sky-high, but to them, it's just play money. It might as well be penny-ante. In this case, you won't be intimidating anyone, or bluffing. These moneymen probably just want to play, so they'll play many hands and call more than fold. You won't bluff them. You'll make money by folding prudently and by showing them a better hand on the river. They'll pay you off. They are the opposite of scared money and too far within their comfort zone.

The Middle Ground

As a solid player, you must be at ease with the stakes, but you want limits high enough to keep you sharp and prevent you from playing too loosely. Play as high as you're comfortable with, as long as the stakes don't make you timid and you don't play with money you can't afford to lose. You will find the good players in this middle ground.

Take this test: If you have not called a bet because you thought about what that money would buy, you are playing too high. If you have not bluffed or bet a hand for value because you thought about the money, the stakes are too high. If you tossed money in because the bet was so low it didn't matter, then you are playing too low.

Most of all, seek a game that is profitable, regardless of stakes. Just because a game has higher stakes doesn't mean you can win more money there.

 Shark Bites

"Everyone, in life and poker, has good points and bad points. One of my good ones is that I don't give a **** about money when I'm playing. That part of my brain is missing."
—Rick Bennet, *King of a Small World*

Taking Control

In Hold'em, it can be argued that the most important bets come preflop. This is where you establish dominance. At the highest level, especially in a small field, this fight for control is key to winning the hand. You have no qualms about betting to whittle down the field to as few opponents as possible. This is in part to make others believe you have a made hand, even if you miss the flop. With your dominance established preflop, betting forcefully on the flop will bring home the bacon, except in the rare case one of your few opponents gets lucky.

Others must know that you will keep betting at them, all the way to the river if necessary. So if the flop comes J-9-7 and they say to themselves, "He can't have hit that flop," your bets will say something different. If they want to call your flop bet and big turn and river bets to find out if you have an overpair ($100 in a $20–$40 game), they are welcome to do so, but they usually won't. You, however, can always call off the attack if you feel your A-Q isn't going to take it this time. You have less at risk than they do.

The Battle for Dominance

If you bet preflop in a serious game, good players may try to take the play away from you by raising. With a few limpers already in, say you raised the blind from middle position and someone puts you on a hand like A-J. He raises. It doesn't matter what he has. It's about the bet now, not the hand. He's playing his stack (you need money for this move), the player (you), and position (he has the advantage). The other players are now folding unless they have a genuine top hand (A-A, K-K, Q-Q, A-K) so you both have gained information.

 **Shark Bites**

As Doyle Brunson writes: "I refuse to let someone keep taking my money. . . . An aggressive player might do it for a while, keep leaning on me. But, at the first opportunity I get, I'm going to take a stand."

You decide not to let him push you around. You haven't picked up superstrong vibes, and if you back off now, he'll do it to you every hand. So you raise back, telling him you have a real hand, even though you actually just have a trap hand. Your A-J is easily dominated by likely raising hands: high pairs, A-K, and A-Q. If he just calls now, you have your answer. You will bet the flop no matter what. If he raises again, he might have taken his quest for domination too far, or he might actually have something this time.

Your knowledge of your player and the flop will determine how far you push this if he takes the last preflop raise. If you pair a hole card, you will of course bet. If he raises, you either fold to his dominance or check-call him to the river. If you don't pair, you still bet. If he raises, you might want to give it up, or check-call to the river, depending on your read on this player. How advanced, how gutsy, is he? How far is he willing to push it?

There are times in a ballsy, heads-up raise-fest when both players have had to turn over absolute trash hands at the river. It's about convincing the other guy—it's not about the cards you hold—because at its core a bet is a declaration: I have a better hand than you!

If you can convince him, then he must passively chase you—or, more likely, give up and fold.

Texas Truths

Seek dominance in most hands you are in, and hope that this will spread to the game as a whole, but you are not going to win every hand. Sometimes you will back off, fold, or call off a bluff. Losing pots late and showing down losing hands doesn't gain respect. Poker is about winning the most money not the most pots.

Getting Respect

To establish dominance, you must be taken seriously as a player. You don't want to be perceived as a chronic bluffer or maniac. For your bets to have respect, other players must believe your bets demonstrate confidence in a threatening hand. You must condition competitors to believe that your bets mean genuine strength, so bet it up with good hands. Bet strongly and take the pot with strong hands. It makes no sense to whine, frown, and act weak and then bet. It doesn't compute and people will smell a rat. It is much better to bet strong when you are strong, and in most cases, this is a sound strategy. It is rare for you to get such a good hand that you welcome callers. More often, you want to win the pot right now. You want people to run away, not jump at the chance to call a foolish bet.

Only then will you be able to open up and grab control, bet on draws, and steal pots.

Your Best Choices

One of the biggest failings of mediocre Hold'em players is that they overvalue calling a bet. They put calling on the value scale somewhere between raising and folding, when in fact it is generally worse than both options. Calling is weak, and good players take advantage of weakness. All a call does is invite further bets and raises against you.

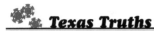

Texas Truths

At high limits, many players say that, in general, if a hand is worth calling a bet with, it is worth a raise. If it isn't worth a raise, it isn't worth a call.

A call is reacting. It isn't pushing the action. You're in a defensive posture waiting to be hit, rather than taking the fight aggressively to the enemy. Sure, there are times to call, such as with a draw and a large field, but for the most part, you want to be in the lead, and bet with the lead.

Calling is the antithesis of dominance. This is why pros get so mad if they have "called off their chips." When you call, you have only one way to win: you have the best hand. But if you are betting, you have two ways to win: you have the best hand, or you force the other players to fold, sometimes with a better hand or potential winner. Good players are always seeking this second way to win. That is why they often fold a hand rather than show weakness and let someone else take control. And folding saves money. Calling, however, often loses it.

Feeler Bets

You know you want to pound on weakness with your bets. You know you use bets to increase your profit when you are the favorite, and you know you use raises, reraises, and check-raises to manipulate the perception of the cards you hold. But bets also can save you money when you are not sure if you are behind in a hand.

Johnny Quads' Corner

The check-raise is a brutal weapon, but it is a two-edged sword. On the one hand, it can double your profit, but it is a dead giveaway that you have a monster. It should be in your arsenal, and players should be aware you will use it, but it doesn't always make you money. It should be used sparingly.

By using "feeler bets," you can sometimes get away from a hand before it gets expensive. Say you raised pre-flop with J-J, and the flop comes with a dreaded ace, A-10-8 rainbow. If you're first to act, you bet, representing an ace. If you're raised, you can now dump the hand, safe in the knowledge that you are beat. If someone else bets first, you might fold depending on if the player is the tricky sort. If you want to be sure, send out a probe—raise her. She will either show weakness or strength. If she folds, great, she should if she doesn't have an ace. If she just calls, you evaluate your player and decide if a big bet on the turn will make her fold, or if she will check/call her ace and weak kicker (or second pair) all the way down. However, if she raises, you have your answer. You can fold before the big bets hit.

Remember in this scenario that the more players seeing the flop, the more chance someone has hit that ace. You must just check or fold those jacks unless you believe you can represent A-K—since you raised preflop—and force others to fold their "weaker" aces.

Blind Man's Bluff

There's the story of the blind, crippled old man sitting in his bedroom in his wheelchair when he hears a burglar jimmy the door to his seedy apartment. The thug rummages through the living room, and by the time he crosses the bedroom threshold, the old man is ready for him. "Don't move," he says firmly, pointing a gun near the doorframe where his ears have told him the punk is.

"Easy, old man," the thug cautions. "Everyone knows the guy who lives here is blind. You'll never hit me even if you had the guts to shoot. Give me the piece and I won't hurt you."

"How do you know I'm him?" replies the blind man, who sees nothing but blackness, but who keeps a firm grip on the pistol and a steely sightless gaze. "And besides, I see well enough. Hear pretty good too. I can't afford to lose a thing. In fact, I have nothing to lose . . . down on the floor. Now or I shoot!"

The punk looks at the wheelchair, the blind man's cane in the corner. "You're blind all right," he mutters. "But I don't know how blind. Maybe you *do* have the guts.

I don't know, but you appear to be holding the cards. You win this one."

The burglar lies down on the floor and the blind man, who couldn't have hit the broad side of a barn, dials 911. He's holding the punk at gunpoint when the cops come. The gun wasn't even loaded, but it didn't matter. The stakes were too high for the burglar to call.

Any Hand Can Win

Bluffing gave the old man a second way to win. The first would be a loaded gun and an adequate set of eyes. The second was making the thief *believe* he had a loaded gun and an adequate set of eyes. Poker is the same, and good players use that second way to win sometimes. You also need to put opponents on notice that at times you will bet with nothing. If you only bet with lock hands, who is ever going to call you? If you never bluff, then a bet from you always means a big hand. The only players who will call you, in that case, are other players with monster hands, or idiots.

 Texas Truths

Every home game has that one supertight player who never bets until he gets the nuts. What happens then? Everyone folds and he wins nothing.

Sitting and waiting for the nuts is no way to win at poker, but there's a fine line you must walk. You want your bets respected because you will need to force folds and isolate, but you also need to get some hands paid off. If you're so predictable that people fold whenever you bet, you're not betting and bluffing enough. And if you never get called when you bluff, you're not bluffing enough. On the other hand, if you're always called, you're too loose and bluffing too often.

Changing Gears

The idea is to keep bluffing (intelligently, of course) until you are caught, then back off, because now you will be called more. This is especially true in low-limit and home games. If you are caught bluffing, that move will resonate for many games to come. No one will forget, and many hands will be paid off. So, forget bluffing for a while, and tighten up.

Shark Bites

"The Watergate cover-up turned into a poker game on a national scale. It was, in an obvious sense, the biggest bluff that Richard Nixon ever ran, the basis of which was that if the full weight and prestige of the Presidency were committed to the cover-up, Congress wouldn't 'see.'"
—David Spanier, *Total Poker*

After you've beaten their brains in with great hands for a while and they start backing off, think about changing gears and bluffing again.

This is all part of keeping opponents guessing and confused about what cards you hold. You don't want them to get a read on you, like that guy who only bets with the nuts. Just like the blind man, you will be taking a risk. Your chips are out there without a net—if you're called, you lose. But without the threat of the bluff, you are an open book. Don't get a reputation as the "table bluffer" or the "table rock." If either one is your image, try to make money by playing against type.

When to Bluff

A bluff has to make sense. You must be representing a made hand, and opponents must believe it is probable you are holding those cards based on your mannerisms and betting actions thus far. Don't just throw chips in and expect everyone to fold. For example, bluffs on the river must often be set up with bets or raises on the turn. For example, the board is 7-6-5-3-2 and you suddenly start raising, expecting people to put you on a straight. But wait, you reraised preflop. They know you and thus know there isn't any hand that you would reraise with preflop that will now give you a straight. Your bluff with A-K failed.

Successful bluffing means proper timing, correctly analyzing your table image, knowing how opponents will react to your bluff bet, figuring out what cards they think you hold, and reading what they have. Simple! Here are some factors to be aware of when considering a bluff:

- **Pot size.** If the pot is large, there is less chance someone will let you take it uncontested.
- **Number of players.** The more people are in the hand, the greater the chance someone will call.

- **Bets and raises.** If someone has already bet, you can expect him to call your bluff. If there's a raise, forget it.
- **Any sheriffs out there?** Some players never let someone take a pot uncontested.
- **Are remaining players timid?** If so, you have a chance; it's the same if they are "thinking" players.
- **Have you shown strength?** Being the leader in the hand might win it for you if no one hits his or her hand strongly.
- **Has a scare card hit?** Sometimes an ace or third flush card is the table's worst nightmare. Bet as though you have it.
- **Do you smell weakness?** Or has everyone checked to you? If so, don't disappoint them. Bet it.
- **Are you a maniac, wild, loose, or always bluffing?** You will be called.
- **Is a big winner tossing in call bets, or a big loser desperately calling?** If so, don't try to buy one.

Remember, you can bluff a savvy, logical, thinking player if you can convince her you have a plausible hand. A bad player will call you no matter what. He has no clue. You'll need a real hand to beat him.

The Power of the Semibluff

The semibluff is an important weapon in your limit and no-limit Hold'em arsenal. You know how essential being aggressive is in limit poker. Well, the semibluff allows you to take control of a hand when you have nothing more than a draw and gives you a fighting chance to win the pot even if you do not make your hand.

Say you have limped in with 10♥-9♥, and the flop comes Q♥-7♥-4♣ or Q♠-J♣-4♦. You have a flush draw or an open-end straight draw. You're about a 2-1 dog in each case. But what would happen if instead of just trying to see the turn and river as cheaply as possible—as opponents would expect you to do with a drawing hand—you raised and reraised and played the hand aggressively?

 Shark Bites

Semibluffing is just one hammer in your toolbox of aggression. As tournament millionaire Phil Gordon writes in *Poker: The Real Deal:* "If there's one *X* factor that unites all great poker players, it's their willingness to play aggressive poker. Like it or not, aggression seems to have a magical effect at most poker tables."

You just might take over and win the pot even if you miss your flush or straight and have absolutely nothing. What you are doing is bluffing with outs, but representing a made hand. Some players might put you on a set or two pair. You win a nice pot if you hit, you might get a free turn card if you want to call off the "bluff" portion of your semibluff, and you sow the seeds of confusion among your tablemates in this hand and hands to come once they find out you will bet aggressively with nothing but a draw.

A strong bet on the flop might mean winning the pot outright on the turn or river if the rest of the field is weak. Try it—just not every time.

The strength of this play, besides confusing foes, is that if the "bluff" doesn't work (someone raises you on the flop or turn), you still have a bunch of outs that could win for you.

If you've learned your aggression and semibluffing lessons well, you'll be ready to tackle tournament poker. Read on.

Chapter 11
The Electric World of No-Limit Tournament Hold'em

With millions of dollars at stake on the turn of a card, no-limit tournament Hold'em is the most cutting-edge and intense brand of poker today. Win a satellite or pay an entry fee as high as $25,000 and you can stare down the best players in the world across the green felt. But be careful. What looks so easy on TV can quickly become a stomach-churning disaster in real life. You'll need more than a buy-in and a pair of sunglasses to win at no-limit.

Fun, Not a Way of Life

Hold'em tournaments, even those with a low buy-in, are adrenaline-pumping, do-or-die competitions that rival the emotional intensity of any athletic competition. Going deep into an event with a chance to take first and pocket big bucks is an unforgettable feeling. But heart-pounding tournament play is no way to make a living, even with the large overlays and huge payoffs provided by the sea of raw newcomers inspired by TV. Very few players can make a go of it playing tournament poker, and there is no guarantee that those "making it" right now can keep it up over time. Most professional players today make their money in everyday cash games—tournaments are just an exciting diversion and hopefully lucrative fantasy, as they should be for you.

Card Questions

What is an overlay?
If you're one of the top 100 players in a tournament with 400 players—but 300 of them have no chance—you are a 99-to-1 shot to win, but if you win, you will be paid much better than 99-1 on your entry fee. That is an overlay and a good bet.

Tournaments cannot be counted on for steady income. They are mathematically brief scenarios in which luck is definitely a factor, especially in shorter events where the blinds rise every forty minutes or less. The faster the event is, the less chance a good player has to use his skills: patience, discipline, reading players, bluffing, and so on. Luck, that random miracle, keeps bad players in their lucky shirts coming back. But good players try to reduce the luck factor, which is why they generally avoid tournaments where the blinds increase too quickly. The more-expensive events take more time (the 2005 WSOP main event, with 5,619 players, took nine days), but with thousands of entries, many of today's top pros believe the best player no longer wins the Big One.

Another point to keep in mind when fantasizing about tournament glory is that they only pay off if you finish in the top 10 percent. So, you can outplay 89 percent of the field, playing tough for hours or even days, and wind up a loser. However, if you outplay 89 percent of your opponents in a cash game, you will win a lot of money. And the big tournament money is only in the top three places.

It's no wonder today's big-name pros hedge their bets with a plethora of books, videos, DVDs, seminars, "boot camps," Web sites, magazine columns, and high-paying online poker-room endorsements.

 Shark Bites

Tournament star Daniel Negreanu on the thousands who now enter the WSOP: "As far as the prestige of winning the event, it's lost some of its luster because every year we're going to see a random guy win. It's no longer an event, in my mind, that crowns the real world champion."

Big Money
Four years ago, Layne Flack was the number-one tournament winner (not including WSOP). He took home $800,000

for the year, but it cost him $450,000 to win it. Entry fees and expenses can eat you up. World Poker Tour buy-ins run from $5,000 to $25,000. Sure, the prize money is much greater these days, and the overlays are huge with all the rookies, but you still must cut down a lot of players to make money.

Beating hundreds of opponents, no matter how weak they are, is a daunting task, and then you must factor in the minefield of hard-nosed regulars and seasoned professionals who will stare you down, peeling you away like an onion. Top tournament specialists enter at least one event a week. Some players compete in more than three hundred events a year! You're not going to be fooling them. So remember that these events are fun: they don't pay the rent unless you want to count on Lady Luck to put food on the table.

Discussion in this chapter refers to no-limit tournaments with no rebuys or add-ons, or rebuy tourneys after the rebuy period has ended. Rebuy tournaments favor those with money to burn. If this is not you, avoid them.

 Texas Truths

The original WSOP tournaments were designed to bring high rollers into town to lose bags of money to the road gamblers in ultra-high-stakes side games.

A Battle for Life

In a tournament, death is final. You do not suddenly pop up with a new life as in a video game. When you run out of chips, you cannot buy more, and all your mistakes are magnified because you cannot reach into your pocket for cash. You are finished. Your entry fee has flown, and you must slink away from the table as the dealer yells, "Player down." Tournament strategy springs from this simple fact: you must survive. Your chips are so precious that any decision to endanger even one of them must be weighed seriously, a balancing act between risk and survival, between going for a larger stack and sudden death, because you can lose it all in an instant. Unlike limit, where you can predict what a hand will cost to call down, in no-limit all your chips are at risk in every hand. So, don't make loose calls.

 Shark Bites

> Risk in the pursuit of chips versus the survival imperative is the tightrope that only the best tournament players walk successfully. As Max Stern says in *Championship Stud:* "Poker is similar to life. . . . At the moment that you understand that you are going to die, you will have a life."

Chips are like your last tank of oxygen as you wait for rescue in deep space. With a full tank, you have some breathing room. You can be patient. You have options. But as your air supply dwindles, each remaining molecule becomes increasingly valuable, because without them, there is no life. Finally, if rescue has not come, your last oxygen molecule has an infinite value.

Since you cannot acquire oxygen in outer space, you will need to act before you are down to that last molecule. You will have to rescue yourself.

Your Chip Stack

Nowhere is the poker axiom "chips are power" more true than in no-limit events, where death is quick and absolute and a single bet puts someone's entire tournament life in jeopardy. Having chips allows you to use all of your skills, if you have enough ammo to work with. A big stack is a heavy hammer you use to threaten and bully, or to wait patiently above the fray for monster cards. A small stack is as desperate as a death row inmate eating his last meal. A fat stack can bust a small stack at any time, but a small stack cannot threaten a big one.

Be Stack Conscious

It is crucial to know at all times how your chip count compares to those at your own table, and in the event as a whole. The average stack will often be displayed on a TV monitor, along with the number of competitors who are still alive and the total chips in play. You also should be able to calculate what the average stack will be at the final table, and you should keep this tidbit of info in the back of your mind.

You can win some borderline hands with a big stack since you have more "risk power." If you have $2,000 in chips, the blinds are $50 and $100, and you raise $300, a player with $700 will be forced to risk more than half his stack just to see the flop. He's going to need a real hand to do that, so you'll be able to steal that $150. If you are raised all-in by this player, you can easily fold or call. Either way, you're still in good shape.

This chopping away at low-risk small pots is one way top players build their stacks. They don't do it by going all-in and getting lucky. They avoid all-ins if possible, because going all-in is a chance to go broke.

 Texas Truths

> To beat hundreds of players these days, you will prob-
> ably have to survive at least one bad beat, and put a bad
> beat on someone else along the way.

A Tournament Concept

One thing you have going for you when you have the chips to enter more pots is that, for most players, because of the survival imperative, in no-limit play it takes a better hand to call a bet than to open (to be the first to raise the blinds). It's one thing to raise with marginal hands like K-J or A-J or A-10 suited or a pair of sevens if you're first in the pot, but just calling with these hands is asking for trouble, because in tournament poker—unless you have a trapping hand like aces or kings—you are looking just to buy the blinds. In most cases, you don't want to be called. It's just too risky. You will rarely have a made hand preflop, and too many bizarre scenarios occur on the flop. You're not seeking a percentage advantage. You want the sure thing, and the more flops you see, the more chance of disaster. There may be times when you will be forced to gamble a bit, but you don't want to if you don't have to. And you certainly don't need to gamble when you have a big stack or when your stack is still much larger than the blinds.

Johnny Quads' Corner

You can't win a tournament early, but you sure can lose it there. Play cautiously at first and pick your spots.

You don't want to limp into many pots (especially if there is a chance of a raise), and when you raise, you don't really want to be called because if you are, the caller will likely have a better hand than you. And you especially don't want multiple players against you. Multiway pots are the exception in no-limit. You do not want anyone flopping a miracle. You want to be able to predict with certainty if the flop has put you behind, and multiple opponents can make even the best starting hand an underdog. The more players there are, the greater the chance someone else will get lucky. Never call bets (especially all-in bets!) from more than one player without an absolute monster hand.

Keep a sharp eye out for those players who are still playing limit side-game strategy. They will not be calling with better-than-usual hands, and they will be limping in, playing loosely and playing draws—all mistakes. Players who consistently chase draws in tournament poker are losers.

Forget "Draw" Poker

Even if you are getting good odds, you rarely want to risk your life on a draw. Do you want to bet your last chip on a four-flush on the flop if you don't have to? You are a 2-1 dog to hit it, but no matter what pot odds you are getting, you're still out of the tournament two out of three times.

With one card to come, you're a 4-1 dog to hit your flush or open-ender. Even if you're getting 6-1 pot odds or more, do you want to risk your last chips with a 20 percent chance? No. The power of high cards and pairs soars in no-limit, while the strength of draws diminishes drastically, so pot odds can become irrelevant.

You don't want to be calling off chips in this game, or check/calling on a draw. If you can't raise, you will usually fold. The only time you play a draw (when you're not short-stacked or overmatched) is if you can bet on a semibluff and expect to win the pot right now, without having to hit your hand.

 Shark Bites

"It can't hurt to monitor one's luck and the general trend of it: How hot or cold you are is a legitimate factor in the decision-making process. . . . Mathematicians tell us that each hand takes place independently of all others. This is good advice to ignore. If things are going badly, back off." —Larry W. Phillips, *Zen and the Art of Poker*

The Second Way to Win

You *must* have that second way to win in no-limit. You want to be the aggressor—the first one in. If you're not first, at least go in raising. Thus the power of the big stack: it is so much easier to be aggressive and take the pot through sheer force. At the other end of the spectrum, short stacks must hunker down and wait for a hand. The more they wait, the more predictable they get.

Beware the Extremes

Being aggressive with a big stack is one thing, but don't be stupid. Don't make a small stack healthy with a dumb move, and most of all, stay out of the way of the other big stacks. They can hurt you. Confine your play to the desperate ones. Keep in mind when you bet or raise that there are two stacks that will call you most often: very big stacks, and very small ones. The big ones can afford it and may put you on a steal, and eventually, the small ones must take a stand, often with less than premium holdings.

 Texas Truths

The first organized series of poker tournaments was held at the Holiday Hotel in Reno in 1968. Two years later, Benny Binion took over the event and moved it to his Horseshoe casino in Vegas, expanded it, and renamed it the World Series.

Good players with small stacks know that if they get much below four times the big blind, they will no longer have the chips to scare anyone. Without that threat, they will lose their second way to win. Keep this in mind when you see a small stack bet out. It may be an act of desperation by a player who knows he doesn't have the luxury of waiting for a killer hand.

Stand Tall

If you are small-stacked, don't wait until you are down to your last few chips to take a stand. Go all-in and try to buy some blinds. Don't let yourself be blinded out or get so low that multiple players can call you with impunity. Every time the blinds increase, your chips are actually worth less. Yes, you must survive, but you can't have a life in tournament poker if you are afraid to die. You must be willing to die, so that you may live. Don't let yourself become the short stack.

Big-Stack Poker

Stealing blinds and stealing pots on the flop when you believe everyone has missed is an essential part of a winning philosophy. In fact, if you steal the blinds just once every ten hands (and do nothing else), you will make the final table.

Being able to put the pressure on is so important that some players will risk their tournament survival to get a big stack. Some believe that having a small stack hurts their game so much that they will chance busting out early trying to double up. In rebuy tournaments, "rebuy maniacs" bet wildly either to build a big stack or to go bust and rebuy.

In no-rebuy events, you still encounter some loose-aggressives pushing the action and buying pots from the more survival-minded denizens in the early going. Many of these wild men will be defeated by rocks who have finally found the hands they have been praying for. Skilled players will eventually defeat the rocks, but a maniac with chips can be a nightmare for even the best of players because of his aggressive play, especially in a short-handed game.

Contrary to the maniac style, however, being tight early and looser late might be a sounder strategy.

Shark Bites

> "Tournament winners combine extremely good judg-
> ment with some lucky breaks. The trick is to survive long
> enough to put yourself in the position to get lucky."
> —WSOP champ Tom McEvoy

In most tournaments today, there are three types of players: shepherds, wolves, and experts. Shepherds carefully watch over their sheep (chips) and try to protect them from the wolves who at some risk are relentlessly attacking their flocks. Though their chips are decimated, shepherds often manage to make the final table. Many wolves die along the way, but the ones who make the final table have big stacks and have a good chance of winning. The expert is much more wolf than shepherd, but she can play whichever style will work against the players at her table and she can change gears to suit the situation.

An example of a successful shepherd is Dan Harrington, facetiously known as "Action Dan," the only player to make it to the final table of the Big One in both 2003 and 2004. The prototypical wolf is WPT superstar Gus Hansen. "Because I mix it up, I am hard to read," he says. "I play my opponent's hand. If I know someone won't commit all of his chips, I just have to bet. The next time, I might bet with the nuts, and players can't tell the difference."

Whether you are wolf or shepherd, lucky or unlucky, and no matter your style or strategy, you will not win a tournament without a tough and fearless image.

Chapter 12
No-Limit Tournaments Part 2: Be Strong

Because you are looking to pick up so many small pots uncontested in a no-limit Hold'em tournament, you must maintain respect at the table. When you bet, you want others to fold, no questions asked. You want them to think you have a hand when you bet, that you are fearless, and that if they raise you, you will make them pucker up like a California prune by raising back or by pushing every last one of your chips into the pot.

Cultivate a Strong Image

It doesn't hurt for players to think you're very willing to go all-in, even though you certainly are not. Early on, if you can go all-in a few times with a lock hand, it will send a message, whether you are called or not, without risking your entire stack.

It is a good idea to vary your play, your starting hands, and your style to keep others guessing, although you may not always have this luxury. What must remain constant is that your bets and raises need to remain powerful and respected. Bet the same way, with the same expression, manner, and vibe, whether you have pocket aces or are on a steal. If you have been stealing a lot, the other players' perception of you may change, and you may be called more or raised. Be alert for this change and tighten up. If you have a tight image, the time is right to do some stealing. Many players deliberately cultivate an ultratight image early so they can steal later.

Johnny Quads' Corner

You don't need the best hand to win a pot in no-limit, just the right bet in the right spot against the right player. You make a bet that a thinking player just can't call.

Make your raises uniform, too. If you are first in the pot, always raise the big blind the same amount to avoid tipping your hand. In a tight game, three times the big blind is a solid bet. In a loose game, four times the big blind is a good idea. Pick one and stick to it.

Some players try to play a pot-odds game in no-limit. If you have the best hand after the flop (top pair/top kicker, two pair, trips) and you want to protect your hand from obvious flush and straight draws, bet more than the pot. Your foe will not have the 2-1 odds needed to call you.

Weakness Invites Raises

Entering a pot meekly invites aggression, and decisions are brutal at these stakes. Good players can smell weakness and won't let you get away with limping in, so you're just throwing money away. If you limp with a hand like A-10 suited and are raised, you must dump it. Much better to raise with it if you're first in, or fold if you're not.

 Shark Bites

"The key to any winning poker strategy is the ability to deceive your opponents while minimizing your opponents' ability to deceive you. . . . It is about hiding strengths and attacking weaknesses."
—David Apostolico, *Tournament Poker and the Art of War*

If you're in the blind with a hand like 8♥-7♥ or A♣-5♣ or 6♦-6♣, you'd like to play these hands if you can get in cheap. Who knows what the flop will bring? Don't bump it up, because if you raise and someone comes over the top, you must fold. These hands can't stand a raise.

With mistakes magnified to the nth degree in no-limit, you don't want to be the one having to make a tough decision. You don't want to be the player who never calls or who always bets, or players can trap you, but in general, you want to be the aggressor. Keep in mind that the first bettor usually wins in no-limit. Make the other guy sweat it out.

Speaking of trapping, using techniques like slow-playing a set on the flop or pocket aces is a viable strategy, as long as it doesn't depart from your normal play. If this is the only time you've ever limped in preflop or not bet the flop when you've raised preflop, then players may become suspicious. If you're superaggressive, then make your usual raise.

Position Is Strength

Since you don't want to face raises in this game, it is crucial that you play position. You want others to act first. For example, if it's heads-up and an ace flops and you don't have one, if you're first, you usually must check. Then your foe puts in an automatic bet, and you are forced to fold, even if she's bluffing. If you bet first and she raises, you just lost a lot of money. But if *she* is first, she'll have to check because of her fear that you might have an ace. Then you bet and steal the pot. If she has an ace and bets it, you can cheaply fold.

A more risky advanced play would be for you to check, letting the other player bluff at the pot, then you check-raise her for a huge bet or all of her chips. Now she will fold unless she has a monster hand like an ace with a very high kicker—and you would know if she had one of those—or if she has a read on you, is a fool, or is desperate. To come over the top to steal the pot with nothing is a gutsy play that you will learn in time. The no-limit game more than any other takes experience and has a long learning curve. You will bust out often—but it's money well spent as long as you learn from your mistakes.

Starting-Hand Power

Position will determine the starting hands you play, along with your desire to enter a pot raising. Here are some guide-lines until you get comfortable. Refrain from playing trash hands as you see some pros do on TV. On these shows, the players are in a short-handed game and must pursue more hands. Remember, the show is edited—you do not see every hand. And while the pros can get away with playing these hands, you can't, because you do not have their experience with the complex play after the flop when you must be able to read players and put them on hands.

 ### *Johnny Quads' Corner*

Don't let starting-hand guidelines make you predict-able. They are a place to begin. Over time, you will learn how to deviate from them depending on your oppo-nents and the game situation. After you gain experience and understanding, you can mix it up.

Keep in mind that since you will be playing heads-up most of the time, it's all about the high cards. Suited cards and connectors have much less value than in limit poker.

High Cards in Position

In early position, open (be the first to raise the blinds) with pocket pairs, aces through nines, and any A-K and A-Q. If you are raised, reraise with aces, kings, and A-K suited—the monster hands—but dump A-Q, tens, and nines. Call with queens, A-K offsuit, and jacks.

In middle position, if you are the opener, raise with the early-position hands plus eights, sevens, sixes, any A-J, any K-Q, and A-10 suited. If you are then raised, reraise with aces, kings, queens, and any A-K. Call with jacks and tens, and fold the rest.

In late position, you can open with all these hands plus the rest of the pairs, K-J, and Q-J suited. If the blinds are weak, of course, you can steal with any two cards. You can call a reraise with more hands in late position: pairs jacks through eights, A-Q, and A-J. You will raise the reraise with aces, kings, queens, and big slick.

In the blinds, you raise with aces, kings, queens, and A-K against a scary early-position raiser, but against later openers, try a reraise with a pair as low as eights, A-Q, and A-J. You can call with pairs down to eights against an early-position opener, and then add the rest of the pairs as the opener approaches the button. You can call an early-position raiser with A-Q, and then add A-J, A-10, K-Q, K-J, and Q-J as the opener approaches the button.

If Someone Raised First

Much of starting-hand theory is predicated on the fact that the later you act in a hand, the less chance there is of someone having a premium raising hand behind you, so you can play more hands.

Remember that you want to be in control of a hand. This makes being the opener so critical. If someone has raised before you (opened), that changes everything. Now you reraise with aces, kings, queens, and jacks, and any A-K, but fold the rest—depending on the player, of course. If he's a maniac, you can play more hands. If he's ultratight, you might even fold jacks. Avoid those horrible dominated hands that can bust you out, like your A-J to someone's A-K, or your nines to someone's higher pair.

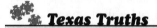

Texas Truths

> In no-limit, you want to live to fight another day when you can get your chips in the pot when you *know* you have the best of it.

Like all decisions in tournament Hold'em, modify these guidelines based on the players you are facing, the size of your stack relative to the field, and the size of the blinds. When you get more experience, you might add suited connectors to your play list. And when play gets short-handed, like at the final table, you must play many more hands and be more aggressive. Always remember that if there is more than one person in the pot before you, it is a sign of extreme danger in no-limit.

Going All-In

If you are one of the better players left in an event, the last thing you want to do is go all-in if you don't need to. You simply don't want someone to get lucky against you, because that would be fatal. Conversely, if you are one of the more inexperienced players, unfamiliar with the intensity and complexity of the moves you will be seeing as the final table nears, you would like nothing better than to get all your chips in before the flop against a good player and try to get lucky and double up, provided you are not a huge underdog. If your competitors are outplaying you after the flop or if their skills are eating away your stack, you might be satisfied to take your chances on what is called a "race."

Common in no-limit, these two-player battles are called races because, basically, they are a coin-flip situation in which one person will get lucky. The classic race is A-K versus a pair of queens or lower. It's about 50-50. You go all-in before the flop and hope to take the pot uncontested, but if you are called, you can still win that coin flip.

What is powerful about going all-in is its courage and finality. Once you're all-in, you've made the ultimate move—no one can outplay you now. They can either fold, or call and pray.

Here are some preflop matchups with their probabilities of winning.

- **Pocket pair vs. lower pair (K-K vs. 8-8):** 82 percent.
- **Pocket pair vs. two overcards (8-8 vs. A-K):** 55 percent.
- **Pocket pair vs. one overcard (8-8 vs. A-5):** 70 percent.

- **Pocket pair vs. lower connectors (K-K vs. 8-7):**
  81 percent.
- **Pocket pair vs. lower suited connectors (K-K vs. 8-7):**
  77 percent.
- **Pocket pair vs. higher suited connectors (3-3 vs. J-10):**
  46 percent.
- **Two overcards vs. suited connectors (A-K vs. 8-7):**
  58 percent.
- **Two overcards vs. unsuited connectors (A-K vs. 8-7):**
  62 percent.
- **Dominating hand (A-K vs. A-J):** 71 percent.
- **One overcard vs. a pair (A-8 vs. J-J):** 30 percent.
- **One overcard vs. suited connectors (A-8 vs. J-10):**
  52 percent.
- **One overcard vs. unsuited connectors (A-8 vs. J-10):**
  56 percent.
- **Two overcards vs. undercards (A-J vs. 8-3):** 68 percent.
- **Pair vs. undercards (10-10 vs. 8-3):** 89 percent.
- **Mixed: Ace-ten vs. king-nine (both unsuited):** 64 percent.
- **Mixed: Ace-9 vs. king-queen (both offsuit):** 58 percent.

What if you are so desperate you must go all-in within the next few hands? Hands that are a coin-flip against a "random hand" are Q-6, K-3, 10-8, and J-7 (all offsuit).

A Note on Bluffing
In limit poker, the turn is often the place to bluff, but in no-limit, the flop is where you make your move. It's also the street where you can send out a feeler bet to gather information. Usually, a bet equal to about 75 percent of

the pot should do the trick in both cases. By betting on the flop, you are putting your opponent (and it is hoped you have just one) on notice that not only will it cost her to call your bet but she will also face bets on the turn and river, possibly for all of her chips. The flop is where both you and your opponent must make decisions. A bet on your part makes her choice easier. No-limit is not a game where you casually see "just one more card" or check/call to the river. After the flop, you're either going all the way with your hand, or you're dumping it.

Scare Cards

It's hard to make a big hand in this game—both for you and for your opponent. If a scare card hits the turn, for example, this is sometimes a chance to steal, depending on your read of your foe's hand. Stealing, of course, is much easier against a single opponent. If an ace, four to a straight, a third flush card, or even an overcard comes on fourth street, a bluff might be in order.

You also need to value bet some marginal hands on the river in no-limit. Not only is that profitable, but it makes you less predictable. If you only bet top hands or a pure bluff on fifth street, when opponents do not put you on a big hand, they will know you are bluffing.

No-limit is about being fearless, but not foolish. Because of the financial pressure you can exert with a big bet, bluffing is an essential tool. Remember that you need an accurate read on the player you are trying to drive out of the pot, or your bluff will only speed your exit.

Shark Bites

> "Reading players is the key skill in no-limit Hold'em."
> —WPT star Howard Lederer

The Human Factor

You will not win in no-limit unless you can figure out what makes your tablemates tick. You must be able to read them like a book and put them on hands, because more than any other game, tournament Hold'em is about people. It's not about the cards—any two cards can win when you make the right move.

Before you bet, call, raise, or fold in no-limit, you must understand your opponents. *They* control how you play a hand. Ask yourself: Who gambles, and who doesn't? Who is experienced, and who is new? Who has only played online? Who is aggressive, and who is timid? Who can be pushed around? Who is the bluffer? Who is in survival mode? Who's pushing the action with borderline hands? Who wants to win the whole enchilada, and who just wants to finish in the money? Most of all, who is loose, and who is tight?

All of these characteristics are magnified in a tournament, and their effect on your play is huge!

There are some good hints on picking up tells in the final chapter, and in *The Everything® Poker Strategy Book*, which makes a good companion volume to this book. Keep in mind, though, that reading players cannot be taught. You must get out there and play. Pay attention, observe, and remember. When you're not in a hand, use that time to study the players and try to put them on hands. Get inside their heads and think about what your strategy should be against each one. If you become proficient, you will develop a feel and an instinct. That is what the top players have and it sets them apart.

 Shark Bites

"If you play by the book, your play will be predictable. No-limit tournament play requires guts and a killer instinct. You need a warrior's mindset."
—David Apostolico, *Tournament Poker and the Art of War*

Food for Thought

You're playing to win money, so don't be that guy who busts out on the bubble (one spot out of the money). While you sometimes can easily buy blinds when the bubble nears because no one wants to be that guy, you must be cautious. It would be a shame to waste hours or days of hard work (and all that buy-in money) by performing a hasty move. If you are short-stacked, get up and check out the other tables; see if anyone is in worse shape than you. Will the shorter stacks have to go all-in on their blinds soon? Can you make it to the money without playing a hand? You don't want to risk your last precious chips unless you have to, and limping into the money could mean hundreds or even thousands of dollars.

If you are disciplined and have the mental and physical stamina for the long haul, you will do well in tournament play. You will find that as an event grinds on, many players lose it. They can't stay focused, and just when you thought it was over for you, someone will bluff off all of his chips and all of a sudden you're in the money. Congratulations!

Important Final Tips

Here are some closing reminders:

- Read the rules sheet that should be available at every event.
- If you are raising, say, "Raise." And say it the same way every time.
- Don't look at your hole cards before it is your turn to act.
- If the blinds are still small, don't take a big risk.
- Bet when you're in the lead and take the pot down right now.
- Play extremely cautiously in early position unless the table is short-handed.
- Don't go all-in preflop with A-K unless you have no choice.
- Play small and medium pairs conservatively unless you're short-stacked.
- Be aware of when you or a foe would be (or are) "pot-committed."
- If betting would make you pot-committed, you probably should go all-in.
- Don't be timid if you're the chip leader—attack with the big stack.

- You never want more than one opponent against you, especially if you're all-in.
- Don't lose your nerve on the turn or river.
- If no one has called you, don't show your cards.

If you are in a huge tournament with hundreds of opponents, don't be intimidated. Just play one hand at a time, and focus on your own table. If you beat the nine players sitting around you, you will do fine.

Luck is a real factor in tournament play, but your skill will decide if that luck will lead to agony or ecstasy. You will surely experience both outcomes if you pursue this gritty, big-bucks combination of championship chess and Russian roulette.

Along the way, at least have the intelligence to restrict your no-limit play to the tournament venue, because until you have a lot of poker under your belt, trying no-limit cash games will only lead to costly misery.

Chapter 13
Internet Poker: Can You Resist?

Online poker rooms are singing a planetwide siren song to new players around the world. Too tired to drive to a casino? Live in the middle of nowhere? Never played before? No matter, as hundreds of thousands of players (gleefully betting millions of dollars a year) have discovered, cyberspace cardrooms can bring the action to you. If you decide to join these stay-at-home card sharks and venture into an Internet casino, be sure to go in with both eyes open.

The Good, the Bad, and the Ugly

Internet poker has proved a godsend for the millions of new aficionados inspired by those high-stakes tournament shootouts on TV. While at one time these rookies would never have had the gumption to enter a brick-and-mortar casino to try their hand against experienced players, today they hop online and at the click of a mouse are in a hand. Online, the early portion of their learning curve is less expensive: there are games for "play money" as well as contests with limits so low (a quarter or fifty cents) that no physical-world cardroom could afford to spread them.

The Good

There certainly seems to be a big upside to online poker:

- You can always find a game, any time of day, every day of the year.
- Changing tables is quick and easy if you don't like your game.
- You can play variations like Draw and Five-Stud that you won't see in casinos.
- You can compete sitting in your underwear with all the comforts of home.
- There are heads-up and short-handed games, which are rare in the real world.
- You can refer to notes and have others help you with a hand.
- Play is twice as fast online, which is great for those who only play a few premium hands.

- The House rake is less, and you don't need to tip the dealer.
- It is possible to play in multiple games at the same time.
- It's great for those who struggle face-to-face because of tells or intimidation.

On most sites, the "lobby" will have a list of current games and tables, along with the stakes, number of players in each game, average pot size, and percentage of players seeing the flop. Whether you like loose or tight, wild action or grinding it out, you can readily find a game that fits your style. And you can observe a table for as long as you like before diving in.

The Bad

With all this convenience can come some problems. For the undisciplined, a poker game waiting in the next room can be a little *too* handy. While going to a physical cardroom takes some planning and anticipation and entails some camaraderie with real human beings, online poker can be a cruel seductress luring the weak away from the responsibilities of life: a spouse, kids, chores, business.

It is far too easy to plop down in front of the monitor at the end of the day and "just play a few hands." Playing while tired or distracted is a recipe for disaster, in the real world or in cyberspace, and online you can lose your stake twice as fast. Low rake or not, at sixty or more hands per hour, the blinds alone can take a toll. Few have the self-control to play a tight, solid game while sitting alone; people don't log on to fold many hands. It's tempting to keep hitting the call button, and bluffing away chips takes no effort at all.

 Texas Truths

In a brick-and-mortar casino, a bluff is a big deal, a gutsy move during which opponents might stare you down. Online it just takes a mouse click—and a click for someone to call you. It is very easy to get in too deep under these conditions.

For many, those onscreen chip icons just don't seem real; your credit-card bill, however, most definitely is.

While it may be a tempting prospect for poker fans looking to earn extra cash in less time, playing multiple games is foolish. It's hard enough to get a line on how the invisible adversaries at your table are playing without trying to figure out *two* (or more) sets of foes. Unless you are attempting the world's tightest strategy (just a select few top hands and that's it), multiple tables won't work.

And don't forget "mis-clicking." this is a common problem among Internet zombies: they mistakenly hit "raise" or "call" instead of the "fold" button, or vice versa.

The Ugly

Whether an individual can legally play Internet poker for money in the United States is still an open question, but the sites themselves are taking no chances; they are all located offshore in the territories of friendly governments that are paid off handsomely. For practical purposes, therefore, online casinos are unregulated. There is no gaming commission (as in Nevada) that you hope is keeping an eye on things. Online casinos make billions (yes, billions) of dollars a year (not all from poker), and they pretty much operate however they want.

Johnny Quads' Corner

Just as in a real-world casino, you must be sharp and completely focused to play Internet Hold'em. The game moves very fast and with information more scarce online, you must pay attention to have a successful game.

There's an old saying around Las Vegas: don't gamble with invisible dice. Yet when you tackle cyber-Hold'em, you are playing for real money with invisible cards against unseen players on an unregulated Web site you can only hope is honest. There's a saying for this in Vegas too: It's called being a sucker.

Texas Truths

Don't expect to read anything critical of online poker. Virtually every author of a book on the subject is affiliated with a poker Web site, as are most of today's name pros and gambling magazines (which derive major revenue from Internet cardroom ads).

People who can come up with poker software can come up with ways to take advantage. While there are scrupulous online poker rooms, it would be naïve to think that they all adhere to a tenet of fairness. The moral is: Internet poker can be fun, but don't bet serious money.

Online Cheating

While the integrity of poker Web sites is uncertain, there is no doubt about the existence of cheating players. Active collusion between players has been a real problem, and the sites say they are working hard to clean up the mess. The most common form is when multiple players share information, either by playing on computers in the same room or by phone. Then they "whipsaw" suckers into submission by raising back and forth when one player has the nuts, with the mark caught in the middle. This can happen in real-world cardrooms too, but there it can be obvious. Online play is so fast that it might be several hands before you realize what happened. The good news is there is a computer record of every cyber hand, so if you smell a rat, take down the hand number and report it (but good luck getting your money back).

 Shark Bites

Michael Sandberg, a college student who in a *New York Times* article claimed to have won more than $90 grand online in a matter of months, credits his alleged Hold'em success to two main principles: know the odds and don't gamble with money you can't afford to lose.

As Gary Carson writes in *The Complete Book of Hold'em Poker*: "Player collusion is a potentially huge problem in online games. . . . It's an ongoing problem that will probably never be completely solved."

This may be one reason that betting limits online are generally lower and high-stakes games are the exception. However, there are a ton of $3–$6 games, which in the real world would be purely recreational. There are reports, however, of people who say they make $50,000 a year or more at multiple $3–$6 Internet games.

Other Collusion

A more passive form of collusion entails several players at a table sharing their hole cards. This is a major advantage when deciding which starting hands to play and putting opponents on hands. This small edge can be huge to an astute player. These cheaters might not whipsaw opponents, but they can fold money-draining, second-best hands that you would play because you don't possess their illicit information.

Hacking has also been a problem for online poker games. The first Internet cash games were spread at *www.planetpoker.com* on January 1, 1998. Within about a year, someone had cracked the random number–generating program used by one site, allowing him or her to know the sequence of cards for the entire deck. Sites now say this is no longer possible.

Texas Truths

Four British players known as the Hendon Mob recently signed a year deal to promote the PrimaPoker.com Web poker room for *$1.25 million*. Almost 30,000 people a day log on to the Prima network.

He, Robot

You also should know that some sites employ shills and prop players, as well as "bots"—robot players that are simply a computer program playing for the House.

It's no wonder that horror stories about bad beats abound. The longshot beats and suck-outs are so common on some sites that it has become a running joke. Someone always seems to catch his flush on the river or two-outer for a set. Some have speculated that if the bot is not outright cheating, then there is a flaw in the software.

With more hands per hour, you would expect more suck-outs, but on some sites, it defies the very laws of mathematics over a long period. The effects of bad beats should actually be lessened when you are playing more hands. If you're going with the odds, your bankroll swings should be shorter lived, and you will approach the expected result faster. However, that is not what folks are seeing with some sites.

Also be wary when taking money off a site (cashing out). There is anecdotal evidence of a well-known syndrome that strikes players who take a profit but continue playing on the site: they are immediately punished with horrible beats.

Without gaming commission supervision, there is no way of knowing if this is coincidence or a scam.

The All-In Swindle

A few years back, this was a major problem, but the situation is improving. Players facing a tough decision simply did not act on their hand. The software then treated them as "all-in," and remaining players built a side pot. This was supposed to protect players who legitimately lost their Internet connection, but it also benefited those who simply wanted a free ride on a draw without having to pay for it. Now many sites have gotten stricter about this, and it is harder to get away with. Find out what your site's policy is. Some will offer no protection during tournament play. Others will give you a quota of "all-in" protections, and when they are used up, you must ask that they be reset.

Card Questions

How can I find online cardrooms?
You can learn what's going on in most Internet poker rooms at ✍ *www.pokerpulse.com*. This site has up-to-the-minute info on what games are being spread in the different rooms and how many players are active on each site.

Do Invisible Players Have Tells?

The reason many top players don't play for big bucks online isn't the danger of cheaters as much as it is the problem encountered when facing invisible players: because reading players is such a crucial skill to successful poker, a good player's advantage is lessened if he or she cannot study you. There is no talking (or lack thereof) or "feel" to a situation and there are no body-language clues, giveaway mannerisms, or any of the other subtleties and tells that will be touched on in the next chapter. An expert who just needs a "flicker" is playing with one arm tied behind his back, and those who use practiced moves of deception to "play the player, not the cards" are also stymied. As your people skills lessen, however, the importance of math grows.

Card Questions

Does playing position matter as much online?
Playing position and pot odds are huge online. Let them guide you. Look to the pot. A good bet is a good bet, online or not.

You need to play a straightforward game online. Nothing fancy. You should use a fairly tight, especially selective, very solid strategy, and most of the techniques and tactics in this book will apply online.

While the perils of online Hold'em are many, don't despair—all is not lost, tells-wise. There *are* a few clues to your online foes.

Chatting It Up

If these are flesh-and-blood people online, find out about them. Use the text-chat function to feel them out. You will be amazed at what you learn simply by observing how they talk. And you will be floored at how many young players there are—high school and even junior high age. At least, you will think so, until they tell you they are in college. Without a lot of prodding you will be able to divine age, poker experience, personality, time at the table, as well as if someone is on tilt, distracted, in multiple games, and winning or losing. This can easily lead to a definitive idea of loose or tight, skill level, and bluffing probability.

Screen Name Revelations

Cyber players choose their screen names, and sometimes the icon or "avatar" that represents them at the computer table. These are great clues. For example, someone might choose a bouquet of flowers to represent her, while another person might choose a fist, a Star Wars character, an animal, or a flag.

Trying to establish a misleading table image is problematic online because players change tables so often (and you're not even sure anyone is paying attention). A screen name can be an easy place to intentionally misrepresent your playing style.

Texas Truths

Take notes on every cyber player you face. This information is invaluable and can be vital when figuring whether to call a possible bluff, and there are many of these online.

I once joined a site where I decided I was going to play very tight, so I took the name "Maniac." I would bet wildly for a hand or two after I joined the game, then tighten up the rest of the night. Needless to say, my big hands were paid off handsomely.

Click Speed

The online game is very fast. There isn't a lot of contemplation time. The speed of online play is another disadvantage for a thoughtful player, but it can be a telling clue if you pay attention. Play with the same players long enough, and you can get a feel for their speed, just as in real life. A variation means something's going on. Unless you are against tricky players (whom you look out for, of course), a fast check means weak, and fast bets or raises mean strength. A long hesitation before checking means weak (he wanted you to think he was going to bet), and a long hesitation before betting means strength.

 Johnny Quads' Corner

Use the play-money games online to learn the site, rules, and button functions. Once you are comfortable with the speed of play and the interface, play for real money.

Players who have preclicked the "check" or "check/fold" buttons have told you something: there was no chance of them betting, and they are extremely weak. Their checks appear on screen with no delay. On the other hand, those who have clicked the "raise any" button have told you they intended to raise no matter what action was taken in front of them. Their raises show up instantaneously.

Getting a Read on Your Table

In general, the quality of play is much worse (and looser) online than in a casino, so good solid play and paying attention should get you the money, but it won't always be easy. Internet poker has fueled the poker craze in high schools and colleges, and while the majority of online competitors are inexperienced and young, they can be very aggressive. Fortunately for the smart player, they are aggressive to a fault and very impatient. They also greatly overvalue their skills. They don't realize how much table time you need at this game to become a skilled player.

Study Your Environment

By watching the hands closely, you should be able to discover who the bluffers are, who is loose or tight, and who is out of their comfort zone. Usually, text-chatting with someone and paying close attention to the way they type will give you clues as to their age. Younger players are either very aggressive (college) or very tight (high school). Patience is how you beat the aggressive ones. Aggressive plays or good hands will beat the tight ones.

Get a feel for the table. You will bluff less, but loose and tight game strategies apply. In a tight game, you can bluff more. In a loose game, bluff less. It should be easier for you to play a tight style with so many more hands per hour. Fold on the flop if you don't have a killer draw or top hand. Don't call off chips. Watch for bluffers, but don't bluff much yourself. Change tables if you're hitting a brick wall.

 Texas Truths

> Avoid short-handed games until you really know what you are doing. You are forced to play many more hands and the bankroll swings can be brutal.

There are online calling stations, maniacs, and rocks galore, but except for those trying to make serious money, there are fewer tight-aggressive experts. Don't forget to keep notes on every player you encounter. You may also request "hand histories" from the site and find out what cards people played, as long as they were in the hand at the showdown. Do it!

Bluffing Online

With the instant-gratification generation as your chief opponents, you can see why so much bluffing occurs in online games—players get bored. They also play while distracted, play multiple games, and, well, it's just so easy to bluff when nobody can see your face.

On the Internet, many more players stay to the river with losing hands (often just an ace) to keep from being bluffed. You can get a feel for a bluff in the real world, but it's difficult online (with few tells and no vibe) so there is a lot of calling. Think about that before you try to buy a pot, and bet right out with your good hands.

Johnny Quads' Corner

Just because there are thousands of mediocre online players doesn't mean that all of them are bad. Pros play on the computer from time to time, and there are serious players trying to grind out a living on the Internet. Stay alert!

Fast Action

Online Hold'em can give you a lot of experience in a short time. Some of that experience will translate to tough, real-world poker, and some won't. For example, single-table, low buy-in, no-limit tournaments online are a good way to get your feet wet, and, in some ways, are practice for the final table of a major tournament. You definitely can get a feel for some of the strategy and betting maneuvers. But they cannot prepare you for being stared down by someone after you have gone all-in on a semibluff.

Online Attributes

Internet players are impatient, weak on finding tells, and ineffective at hiding their own when they switch to the physical world. You will often see these uncomfortable players hiding behind hats, hoods, CD players, and sunglasses. If you are facing an Internet player, act accordingly. She is used to making quick decisions and quick moves. Think about what she is good at and what she lacks; don't be hasty. Wait for a mannerism to give the bettor away. She is not used to waiting, being idle, or sitting still. Let your intuition take over, and wait her out.

 Texas Truths

Internet and younger players tend to drastically overvalue the small and medium pocket pairs. In no-limit, these can be horrible trap hands that call for a lot of finesse, discipline, and experience to be played correctly.

Online Satellites

One place where the online game excels is the satellite tournament. A big reason real-world tourneys are setting entry and prize-pool records all over the country is the growing number of online qualifiers. Rookies as well as some top players are using the Internet to win cheap entries into WPT events or the WSOP everyday. World Series entries tripled from 2003 to 2004, largely due to the Internet, and in both years, the winner qualified in a cheap super satellite on *www.PokerStars.com*. Today they are millionaires, but they didn't do it by walking up to Binion's and plunking down $10,000.

Internet poker is definitely here to stay. Fortunately, a side effect of the online play is a big surge in attendance at brick-and-mortar casinos. Poker rooms are opening and expanding everywhere, broadening the sea of green felt for you to test your skills.

Chapter 14
Poker in a New Millennium

The beauty of poker is in its psychology. The best hand doesn't have to win, but the best player usually will. Develop a feel for the game and the players you stare down around the green cloth, and you will accomplish your mission: to win money and have fun. Besides, the lessons you learn at the table will help in every facet of your life. Just try not to lose the "fun" part of your goal as you pursue poker wealth.

Spotting Liars Through Tells

As your skills grow, you will seek out higher-limit games to make more money. As the stakes increase, you will battle more skillful foes and face fewer players just praying for lucky breaks. Betting skills and your ability to read players will win you the money in these games. Being able to put someone on a given pocket hand through observation of his style and personality is crucial. Watch everything—and remember it all.

The good ones can get a feel for a player that becomes ESP-like. They can correctly answer the question: does she have me beat, or doesn't she? Players without this skill must try to grind it out at lower limits playing a strictly mathematical game. Those who have the skill are success-ful at high stakes and no-limit and can even discover that most devastating of clues: the tell.

What Are Tells?

A tell is something a player does (or fails to do) that unintentionally gives away his personality, playing style, or (especially) the cards he holds. Tells come in the form of mannerisms, body language, gestures, movements, facial expressions, a break in routine, changes in voice, or just about anything. They are especially discernible when a player handles her chips or cards, speaks, or betrays an intense interest (or lack thereof) in a hand.

Tells can be involuntary physical responses to stress, such as a shaking leg, or deliberate attempts to mislead, such as slamming down chips too confidently during a bluff bet. You discover tells by acting as a human lie detector.

First, observe or talk to a player when he is himself (not in a hand), and then compare this to his demeanor under stress (actively involved in a hand). Look for changes. Changes in good players are subtle or undetectable, but in average players, these differences might be obvious. Next, look for differences between when the player is bluffing and when he has a can't-lose hand. How does he act with a draw versus a hand like top pair on the flop? How does he act when he might win but is not a lock? Look for consistencies and patterns over time.

 Johnny Quads' Corner

A dog can't help wagging his tail when he's happy. If you grab the tail, his body will shake. Many players who try to hide their emotions have the same problem.

Tells Hide Deception

From your very first hand, poker became a game of hide and seek. You couldn't let people know your cards, or you would surely lose, just as if you knew others' cards, you would always make the correct decision. The first time you were dealt a good hand, dollar signs went off in your brain, but you had to resist the urge to smile and cheer—as you would if you scored a goal in soccer—or you would make no money. When you received your first bad hand, you were upset, but you could not show it, or you would give yourself away and be run over. You were forced to hide your emotions and be deceptive. To be honest would make you transparent and predictable.

So from Hand One, you were lying. You sometimes want your opponents to perceive your big hands as weaker than they are so you get paid off, and you always want your medium and bad hands to appear stronger than they are—especially in tournament play where you must steal some pots. A bluff is a theft, and nothing more than a bald-faced lie. In all but the most experienced players, this falsehood creates discomfort and stress, which manifest in the body.

Card Questions

How can pros be so calm when risking huge sums on a stone-cold bluff?
They are comfortable with their decision. Win or lose, they are convinced they made the right move and can live with the result, so their demeanor is relaxed and natural.

Realize that opponents react to stress differently, but there are patterns. Once you have discovered some stress changes, then observe to find out what they mean. Some people react the same way when they have a huge hand they want paid off as when they are on a stone bluff. Others don't.

Involuntary tells include shaking torsos, sweating, dilating pupils (great card!), throbbing jugular vein (excited), holding of breath, hoarse voice, and trembling hands (monster hand). If nothing else, these are all signs of extreme interest. It is up to you to figure out if subterfuge is involved. Sometimes these tells just give away a lock hand.

People used to think a trembling bettor was on a bluff, but usually it means the opposite. Be on the lookout for breaks in routine such as a sloucher suddenly sitting up very straight or a constant talker who is suddenly quiet.

Clues Everywhere

Just as you can get an indication of someone's personality through dress and hairdo, you can also pick up clues to playing style. If someone keeps his chips in a jumbled mess, this often indicates a loose player. Someone who carefully organizes her chips in stacks of twenty with the markings all lined up on the side is definitely a mathematical player with a plan. Players who only seem happy when raising are aggressive players or maniacs, while those who seem in pain when they must raise are calling stations.

Deliberate actions can be tells if you know how to interpret them. A player who slams his raise down with extra force may be acting strong when he is weak—a very common play. Or he could be crossing you up by acting strong when he really *is* strong. This is when knowing your players saves the day.

Johnny Quads' Corner

If you see a player grab his chips before it's his turn and act as though he is going to bet (or call a bet), that is a sign of weakness. He wants to discourage a bet, so you should bet into him. You want to do the opposite of what the other guy is trying to manipulate you into doing.

Acting weak when strong and strong when weak is an obvious tell in new players. Watch for the player who acts disappointed and then raises or check-raises. You should fold your hand immediately.

In the same way, inexperienced players will act disinterested in a hand when they have the nuts, often looking away and doing everything to avoid eye contact. They are trying to say, "I am not a threat." However, when they have nothing, they might stare you down to keep you from betting or calling a bluff. Players who are aware of these well-known tells might do the opposite or, more likely, just act natural and identical no matter what cards they hold.

Using Tells to Detect Bluffers

Since bluffing is deceit, you can sometimes identify conflicted players through some classic lying clues:

- Hands around the face or mouth, touching the brow or hair, or crossing arms and/or legs.
- Talking fast and telling you to hurry up. He can't take the anxiety.
- Being overly friendly. She's your pal. She wouldn't lie.
- Yawning, licking the lips, touching the nose, or swallowing excessively.
- Avoiding eye contact. Be careful of this one—everyone is aware of it.

These tells are a starting point. You will need to discover your own. Many tells are unique to a specific player, such as the woman who always puts her cigarette down when she has a great hand or the guy who can't help betting extra forcefully and verbally when he knows he has a lock. Pay special attention to players when they first look at their cards, and when they put chips into the pot.

Everyone asks: Do I need a "poker face"? Not if you think a poker face is an emotionless, robotic mask. What you need to be is comfortable, relaxed, and natural. Natural is the key. Be "one" with your decision, and be yourself. Pros are not stone-faced, but they don't give anything away. What's important is that you are consistent whether you have the nuts or just a busted flush and that your actions don't allow someone to get a read on you. The more movement and talk, the more chance of a tell, but being a statue can be a tell as well.

 ### *Texas Truths*

An old poker proverb says, "If you know how a man plays poker, you will know the man." But conversely, if you can figure the man out, you will know how he plays poker.

Guard Your Bankroll

By now you know that money is power in this game, and that a smart player never plays with scared money. Serious players, even if they only play a few times a month with pals, maintain a poker bankroll. It makes things a lot simpler, especially if you are married. You have a separate fund for poker: your winnings go into it, and your losses (and only your losses) come out of it. Playing with cash earmarked for necessities is a losing way to play.

Bankroll Size: How Much Is Enough?

If you are a recreational player, you can risk up to 10 percent of your bankroll on a given night. Say you play in a $50 buy-in affair but are prepared to plow up to $200 into the game if you're having a bad night. In this case, your bankroll should be $2,000. If your bankroll diminishes, so should the amount you are willing to risk in a given session.

To a professional, the bankroll is sacred. Without it, she is unemployed, and no decent pro would ever risk 10 percent in a single session. Even 5 percent is pushing it. An everyday player's bankroll must be able to withstand weeks (even months) of losses, because losing streaks happen to the best of them.

 Shark Bites

"I feel my skill at poker is good enough collateral for a bank loan."
—Johnny Moss

To play $4–$8 regularly, a pro needs at least a $3,000 to $4,000 stake to make his $8 to $12 an hour. For $10–$20, a minimum of $8,000 to $10,000 is needed (we hope) to make $20 an hour, and for $20–$40 no less than $15,000 to $20,000 to try for perhaps thirty bucks an hour. Note that this is bankroll only. A pro also needs a year's worth of living expenses (including insurance) in a separate account, because the bankroll is just for cards. During the year, he must win enough to pay the following year's expenses and grow the bankroll to protect against losses. A poker bankroll should always be moving forward.

You should play at whatever limit is most profitable for you, as long as you have the bankroll to cover it (10 percent amateur, 5 percent pro) and can fearlessly play your best game within your comfort zone.

Turning Pro?

Despite the TV publicity about the glamorous life of tournament professionals winning millions, they are exceptions in the extreme. Many "pros" are grinders who are slowly and inexorably losing their bankrolls and have lost the joy of the game. They are an unhappy lot who don't just want to win; they *must* win. This can severely hurt someone's game, mental outlook, personality, comfort zone, and profit. All that needs to be said about this is: why would you want to turn a game you love into a job you hate? Having a second source of income is a much better way to go.

Leaving a Winner

When should you call it a night? Well, if you're in a game with friends, you're supposed to be there for the fun, not just the cash. So, you're obligated to stay until the game breaks up, unless you've blown your stake or announced an early exit at the beginning of the night. In a casino or online, you can quit whenever you want and get your cash with no hassle—that's one of the things you're paying for. But when, exactly, should you quit?

When to Throw in the Towel

If you've lost two buy-ins, that might be time. Three, for sure. You could be having a bad night, or the game might be too tough to beat. Whatever the reason, in poker, it's best to live to fight another day rather than kid yourself and see a moderate loss become a wallet-busting disaster. There are usually good reasons you're losing, and you may not be aware of them, that's why you should set a "loss limit" before you sit down—and stick to it. You could be on tilt, or the table target. You could be tired, distracted, or concerned about problems at home, with a significant other, or your job. Playing drunk, sick, disturbed, worried, or depressed is a recipe for disaster.

Quit While You're Ahead?

But what if you're way up? Many top players say it is misguided to quit while you're winning, but these players are going to get up and play again the next morning. They play every day, so it's all just one big long game to them. There is no quitting. They say leave a game only if it is no longer profitable. Trouble is, some play so long that they go on autopilot and don't realize when the game has changed. A game they were beating when they were sharp four or eight or twelve hours ago might be much tougher with less focus. It is very hard to maintain sharpness over a long period.

Johnny Quads' Corner

If you're way ahead, why change your style? Just keep doing what won you that mountain of chips. If you suddenly tighten up, you will be predictable. If you start taking chances with money, you might not have it for long. Only game conditions should dictate a change in strategy, not the size of your stack.

If you don't play every day, it's a good idea to set a win goal, and when you reach it, seriously ask yourself some questions. A good benchmark is a hundred times the big blind(i.e., $400 in a $4–$8 game). If you hit this level, have been playing under four hours, are still sharp (be honest), and weak players are still pouring Benjamins into the game, then consider staying.

But that scenario would be the exception. More often, you might be getting tired. If you haven't taken any breaks, your concentration is definitely waning. If you're a big winner, it isn't just skill—you've probably had some luck as well. Streaks don't last forever. And most important, the weak players you fed on have probably busted out and been replaced by some rough players who are targeting your big stack.

Booking a big win is a tremendous boost for your confidence, and your game. There's nothing like going home a winner. Early in your poker career, book some wins. Get used to winning. Being way up and then losing it back is a horrible feeling, and it happens all too often. Go home with your pockets full of green and the next time you hit the table, you'll sit down fresh—and a winner.

A Poker Parable

Hang around California poker rooms long enough and you'll hear this tale that many swear is true: Back in 1930s Los Angeles, a high-stakes home-game operator was raided by the cops. Because he'd been busted so often, he knew in his heart that this time he was facing some serious prison time. Seemingly caught dead to rights, in desperation he came up with a brilliant defense: He would plead not guilty and argue that the game does not violate the state's gambling laws, because poker is a game of skill not chance.

During the trial the prosecution presented its seemingly ironclad case, while the defense stuck to the contention that although money changed hands, poker wasn't gambling. When the case went to the jury, the jurors did a little experiment: They split into two groups, called for cards, and played a little poker. Half a day later, the foreman called for a vote. Eight jurors said poker was a game of chance; four said it was skill. Since a verdict required a unanimous vote, they played on.

Finally, after several days of play, the vote remained unchanged: Four voted for skill; eight said it was just a chancy gamble. The foreman had to tell the judge it was hopeless: The jury could not reach a decision. After the judge announced the deadlock, reporters swarmed the jury, wanting to know about the game. Curiously, there were eight losers and four winners. The losers had all voted poker a game of chance. Not one would admit to being outplayed: It had to be the cards!

The parable's lesson is: Only losers say it's luck. Good players do not blame their losses on the gods—or on Lady Luck.

What to Do If You Are Losing

If you lose big when you lose but win small when you win, you need to ask yourself if poker is for you. Are you comfortable with the game? Do you have an understanding of what constitutes a good hand in different situations? Do you have the talent, smarts, and temperament for Hold'em? As with any sport or endeavor, many people will never be good. If this is you, you must ask yourself if your losses are worth the fun you are having, and if the losses are affordable.

Hang in There

If you are new to the game—that means just a year or two—don't give up. Read, observe good players at work, and play in low buy-in one-table tournaments online. Are you learning from every hand, as you should, or have you fallen into a rut? Are you trying to read players, or just playing by rote? Are you playing just your own cards, or what others don't have? Are you selectively aggressive, or are you more like one of the less-desirable types discussed in Chapter 9? Are you predictable?

A good way out is to ask the best player in your group for help. If you're in a casino, find out who the good players are. Ask them to watch you play or sit in with you. Get their opinion. You might have to pay them for this service, but it's worth it.

Shark Bites

"I hope you'll play right and wager well, unless you're in my game, in which case I hope you'll play like a dummy and throw away all your money to me."
—Johnny Chan

How to Turn It Around

You don't have to be a world-class player to win at this game, just better than your opponents. Sometimes becoming a winner is as simple as playing in a different room against different players. Find players you can beat, and keep improving.

Analyze your play. Do you do better in a loose game, or a tight one? Against seasoned players, or rank amateurs? Maintain records to keep yourself honest. Include wins and losses, venue, type of game, stakes, and time at the table. Track your river bets and calls; you should win most of them. And of course, keep a log of player tendencies if you play with the same group.

Here are some other ways to turn losing into winning (extrapolated from previous chapters):

- Tighten up. Look for reasons to fold, not reasons to call.
- Don't play second-best starting hands. They usually end up second best.

- Don't play too many hands for too long—the classic rookie mistake.
- In a home game, bluff only until you are caught, then tighten up.
- Avoid hands you cannot play aggressively, unless the game is ultraloose.
- Modify strategies and tactics for loose and tight games. Adapt to the players you're facing.
- Cultivate a table image that is the opposite of how you intend to play.
- Vary your style to keep from being predictable, especially if you play with the same group.
- Make more with your good hands. Bet it up strongly with the lead. No free cards!
- Don't get "married" to a hand. Even good hands can be beaten. Lay it down.
- Winning the most pots isn't important. Just win the most chips.
- You don't need to "protect" chips you've already tossed in. If you're beat, fold.
- Be friendly, especially to the players on your left who can raise you.
- Don't make enemies at the table. Winning is hard enough.
- Don't overdo fancy plays like slow-playing and check-raising in an average limit game. You don't need them.
- Unless you have a mortal lock, don't lure players into the pot by slow-playing.

- Don't bring a significant other to the game to watch you. He or she will be bored, and it will hurt your play.
- Maximize money in the pots you win, and minimize money in the pots you lose.
- Average players expect you to play just like them. Bluffers assume you are bluffing, conservative players expect you to have a real hand.

Lastly, reread this book from time to time. Many of the concepts presented here only become clear over time. Skill doesn't come overnight. WPT star Howard Lederer played $2 limit poker for two years—and lost—before he got the hang of it. Go out and play!

Johnny Quads' Corner

Remember, folding trouble hands others would have played and lost with saves you money. This money saved is the same as money won. Folding is as important a skill as any other part of your game.

Poker Will Test Your Spirit

Hold'em can play with your head because if you make a good play on the green felt, you usually only gain a theoretical advantage visible over time. Let's say that through your skillful tournament play, you induce a player with pocket nines to call your all-in bet against your pocket kings. You have achieved your goal: all your chips in the pot with the best hand by far. That is what good players hope for. Through manipulation, betting, and knowledge of your opponent, you are an 80 percent favorite. If you started heads-up, you have gained a 30 percent advantage, and your foe has lost 30 percent. But in reality, you have won nothing! You still could lose the hand. And you will, one hand out of five.

 Shark Bites

"Good poker is hard work.... Great poker is courage."
—Rick Bennet, *King of a Small World*

It's like in basketball when a player sets a pick to free up a shooter. He has gained an advantage because the shooter now has a better chance of making the shot and scoring, but no points have been scored. The advantage is theoretical, a percentage that often only manifests itself over time.

In Hold'em you're not just playing against others, you're playing against yourself. With every tough decision, you are learning about yourself, testing yourself, finding out what you are made of. Through this white-hot crucible of choice and chance, you acquire skills that will aid everything you do in life. Skills like maintaining patience and determination, bluffing, creating a persona, discovering courage, and reading people. And most important, you're having fun doing it and meeting some good people in the process. If you make some friends and contacts along the way, you are a winner. Remember, this is a "people" game!

If you can endure what Hamlet called "the slings and arrows of outrageous fortune," then poker can forge you into a better, stronger, more intuitive person who will be more successful at any challenge or endeavor and at life in general.

But if you can't handle it, if losing tears you up and winning brings little joy, then, whether you are ahead or behind, the game may not be for you. As Jesse May wrote in *Shut Up and Deal*: "People think mastering the skill is the hard part, but they're wrong. The trick to poker is mastering the luck."

Texas Truths

The Venetian hotel/casino in Las Vegas had a revenue of $95 million during the first *quarter* of 2005. It won 24 percent of all chips bought at table games such as Blackjack and roulette and had an average win of $6,100 a day at each of its 134 tables. Aren't you glad you are playing poker instead of trying to beat the House?

Love the Game

Some grinders scoff at those who say they're having "fun" at the poker table. They view them as weak. But if you're not enjoying yourself, why not get a real job? Wasn't enjoyment and excitement the reason you took up poker? Didn't you turn "pro" because it was not a daily grind, not a dreary, mundane, and predictable business?

If you have lost the fun aspect, you need to ask yourself what you are doing with your life. If you can have fun *and* make money, if you have the evenness of temperament to withstand brutal bad beats from people who by rights should have folded and given you the pot, then you are a poker player. If you can realize that those bad beats actually are your bread and butter, that your money comes from plays like that, then you are a poker player. If you can stare poker death in the face without flinching, even if your entire bankroll or tournament life is at stake, then you are a poker player. You are a poker player if you can remain stoic and the master of yourself in the face of a humiliating loss, instead of melting down as one household-name pro did in a well-publicized major TV tournament, where he mumbled the embarrassing pronouncement: "If it wasn't for luck, I'd win every one of these things."

Johnny Quads' Corner

If you cannot only enjoy your winning but also make those who lost to you feel as though they got their money's worth and had a good time even though they might have fattened your wallet, then you are a poker player.

The real pros are those players who win and still make lesser players feel good and want to play the game again. The best players truly love the game.

Your Lifelong Poker Game

Ted Thackrey Jr. in *Gambling Secrets of Nick the Greek* wrote of Nick Dandalos, who spent his entire life fighting the good fight against the gods of risk: "He played incessantly, passionately, joyfully, and always for high stakes; not as a business or a profession, but as truly devoted monks must pray . . . as a kind of prolonged ecstasy."

Whether you end up competing for thousands of dollars or quarters, on TV or just on your kitchen table, this game can capture you, heart and soul—as it did Nick—but each hand is a skirmish, and every game a battle in the larger war that is the tally sheet of your lifetime on the green felt. If, when you have played your last hand, you are ahead, then you are a winner. But poker is so much more than a balance sheet. If it was only about money, you will have spent many hours in a hollow pursuit.

If you bring joy to others around you at the table (other than by giving them your hard-earned cash), make genuine friends, take pleasure and knowledge from the camaraderie and inspiration and stimulation from the game, divine secrets about others, yourself, and life, then you will truly have accomplished something.

May I see you, someday, at the final table. Good luck!
Well, luck really has little to do with it, right?

Appendix A
Hold'em's Cousins

A few poker variations bear a striking resemblance to Texas Hold'em, and they are loaded with action and a blast to play. Be wary, though, because the average winning hand is much higher. Omaha High (commonly referred to simply as "Omaha") and Omaha Eight or Better (Omaha 8/b) are extremely popular and can be found everywhere. What these games have in common are huge bankroll swings and, unlike Hold'em, someone nearly always has the nuts against you.

THE EVERYTHING TEXAS HOLD'EM BOOK

Omaha High

Omaha is dealt exactly like Texas Hold'em except each player receives four hole cards instead of two. This gives a player six possible two-cards hands. In a ten-person game, that's sixty starting hands out there, so anything can happen. The fine point to Omaha is that a player must use two of his or her hole cards to make a five-card hand—no more and no less. Omaha and Omaha 8/b are the only games with this stipulation.

So, if you are dealt four of a kind, that's bad. All you have is a pair that will never be trips. If you are dealt four to a flush, that's worse than if you were dealt only two. If you are dealt two pair, all you have is one pair plus three board cards.

Omaha High: Brief Overview

As far as starting hands, pairs of aces, kings, and queens are great, of course, but preferably suited with another card, as in A♠-A♥-10♠-10♥ or K♠-K♥-10♠-9♥. A high pair with a straight draw is also good, and much better if suited or double suited, as in K♠-K♥-Q♠-10♥. Four to a high straight (a "wrap") is good, and again, much more so if double suited, as in 8♠-9♣-10♠-J♣ and 10♣-J♠-Q♠-K♣. Look for hole cards that work together in multiple ways. A pair of aces with anything is strong, just don't get married to the hand. In fact, don't get married to any hand in Omaha.

Omaha forces you to chase draws, so playing pot odds and knowing the math is essential. The best-case scenario is to the have the best hand on the flop—and to be drawing to the nuts. A set might be best on the flop, but it won't stay that way. You want to be drawing to an ace-high flush or nut straight and nut full house as well. Note the word *nut*. The field of battle is littered with the bodies of those who drew to queen-high flushes and second-best straights. Nut flushes are powerful in this game, but if the board pairs, you're facing a full boat.

Omaha Eight or Better

This high-low, split-pot variation is actually more popular than its high-only cousin. It is dealt like Omaha High, and you still must use two hole cards, but now you use two to make your high hand and, if you wish, a different two for low. The trick is that the low must be five cards eight or below, unpaired. Straights and flushes do not count against the low and the best low is a wheel, 5-4-3-2-A, which is also a straight. If the board does not include three low cards, there cannot be a low hand, so the high hand takes the whole pot. Low hands are read from the highest card to the lowest, so an "eighty-six" low of 8-6-4-3-A beats an "eighty-seven" low of 8-7-3-2-A. Eight-six is lower than eight-seven.

Here are the probabilities of making a low:

- **With four low cards in the hole:** Preflop: 49 percent; if two low cards flop: 70 percent; if one low card flops: 24 percent.
- **With three low cards in the hole:** Preflop: 40 percent; if two low cards flop: 72 percent; if one low card flops: 26 percent.

- **With two low cards in the hole:** Preflop: 24 percent; if two low cards flop: 59 percent; if one low card flops: 16 percent.

To figure the best possible low hand, find the three lowest cards on the board and determine the two lowest hole cards that would fit with those three, without pairing them. Example: If the three low board cards are 8-5-2, you have the nut low with 3-A in the hole. But if a three hits the board, your three has been counterfeited (see Appendix B for more information on this term). The nut low would now be 4-A, making 5-4-3-2-A.

In Omaha 8/b, your best hands are those with a chance to win both ways ("scoop the pot"), such as A♥-A♣-3♥-2♣.

Crazy Pineapple and Tahoe

Crazy Pineapple is a Hold'em variation with a few twists. It is dealt and bet like the standard game, except players receive three hole cards and after the betting on the flop, one of the hole cards is discarded. You do not have to use both hole cards to make a hand. Because of the extra starting hole card, flushes, full houses, and straights are common. This is a less-strategic, "crazier" game than standard Hold'em. With three hole cards to start—a 50 percent increase—anything can happen.

There are two games similar to Crazy Pineapple, so be aware of which three-card variation you are playing. In straight Pineapple Hold'em, you must discard a hole card preflop, before the first bet. In Tahoe, you keep all three to the showdown—but you can only use a maximum of two. Tahoe and Crazy Pineapple are sometimes played high-low.

Criss-Cross

Also called Iron Cross, Criss-Cross is a home game that creates pots. Each player is dealt four cards down, and then five community cards are placed face-down in the shape of a plus sign in the center of the table. After a round of betting, the cards are turned up one at a time starting with the top card and proceeding clockwise, with a betting round after each. The center card is turned up last. This yields two rows of three cards. Players may use one row or the other to complete their five-card hands. One, two, or even all three cards in a row may be used to make a hand. This game can be played high only, but it is better high-low. In high-low, players may use one row for high, the other for low if they wish.

Originally, players received five cards, but the hands became ridiculous. Today, it is mostly played with four cards. When combined with one of the rows, players have a seven-card hand, which puts them on more familiar ground. The game plays much like Omaha. It may also be played with just two hole cards, and then it resembles Texas Hold'em.

Double Board Hold'em

Similar to Texas Hold'em, Double Board Hold'em has two separate boards! There is a flop, turn, and river for both boards, and they are dealt simultaneously. Players make their best hand for each board at the showdown. Players do not have to indicate which board they are using.

The game can be played as winner-take-all, with the best hand on either board taking the whole pot, or as a split-pot game, with the winner of each board getting half the pot.

Other Variations

Cincinnati is played like standard Hold'em except players receive five hole cards.

Blind Man's Bluff is Hold'em except that everyone can see all the hole cards except his or her own. (Cards are usually held on the player's forehead!)

Manila is played with a stripped deck of aces down to sevens (32 cards), so a flush beats a full house. Players are dealt two hole cards; then five community cards are turned up, one at a time, with a betting round after each. The first bet occurs after players receive their hole cards and one community card is displayed. Players must use both hole cards and three community cards to make a hand. Manila is dealt in Australian casinos.

Have fun with these crazy games!

Appendix B
Talk Like a Texan: Glossary of Hold'em Terms

action—Gambling, as in "He loves to be in action." Also: A lot of betting, as in "The action was wild in that Omaha game." Also: It's your turn, as in "The action's on you."

add-on—Additional chips that may be purchased at the end of the rebuy period of a poker tournament.

all-in—A player betting all his remaining chips. "I'm going all-in," or "I am all-in."

bad beat—To make a "sure thing" hand, only to be beaten by a longshot draw.

bankroll—Money a player has to gamble with.

behind—Someone who acts after you in a betting round. "I had a dangerous player sitting behind me."

behind the money—Having the player or players with the most chips acting before you in a betting round.

Benjamin—A hundred-dollar bill (named for Ben Franklin, whose portrait appears on it).

best of it—To have the odds with you.

big blind—The larger of the two forced "blind bets" in community-card games, located two to the left of the button. The big blind is usually equivalent to the maximum single bet on the first round. "Big blind" refers to both the bet and the person making it.

big hand—A really good hand.

The Big One—The $10,000 buy-in no-limit Hold'em tournament at the World Series of Poker that is considered poker's world championship.

big slick—Ace-king in the hole.

blank—Community card that looks like it could not possibly help anyone's hand.

blind—Money put in the pot by a player or players to the left of the button before receiving cards. A forced, "blind" bet.

bluff—A bet made representing a good hand, when in fact the player has a poor (or drawing) hand.

board—The face-up cards on the table used by all players to make their hands. Also: The face-up cards in a player's hand in a stud game.

boat—A full house. Also called a "full boat."

brick-and-mortar casino—A casino in a real, physical-world structure, as opposed to cyberspace. "Bobby is a good brick-and-mortar player but not so good online."

broadway—An ace-high straight.

the bubble—The spot that is one out of the money in a tournament. "I finished on the bubble."

busted—Broke. Also: To lose all one's chips and be out of a tournament. "I busted out." Also: A draw that did not get there; for instance, a busted flush.

button—In a casino, the round plastic disc that denotes which player is the "dealer." The casino dealer gives cards to the player to the button's left first, the button last.

buy-in—The amount of chips a player must purchase to enter a poker game; or, in a cash game, the amount he or she must put on the table to be allowed into the game.

buying pots—To win a hand through a bluff bet rather than better cards.

call—To put the same amount in the pot as another player bet, thus remaining in the hand. "I call your bet."

calling station—Weak player who calls other players too often and rarely raises.

case card—The last card of a rank left in the deck. If three aces are on the board and a player receives the fourth one, she has been dealt the "case ace."

chasing—Staying in a hand with lesser holdings than your opponent's, hoping to make a winning hand.

check—To not bet when it is a player's turn to act.

check-raise—When a player checks and then raises someone who bet after that check.

checks—Poker chips.

community cards—Cards on the board that are shared by all players in games such as Texas Hold'em and Omaha. All players can use the community cards to complete their hands.

connectors—Two or more cards in sequence; for example, in Hold'em, having a jack and ten for hole cards.

counterfeit—In Omaha Eight or Better, when the board pairs one of your low cards.

cracked—To lose a hand you were favored to win. "He caught a flush on the river and cracked my pocket aces."

crying call—A very reluctant call of another player's bet.

dime—One thousand dollars.

dog—Same as underdog. A player not favored to win.

dominated—To have someone's hand beat due to shared cards. For example, in Hold'em, one person has A-8 and another has K-8. The K-8 is dominated because the ace is higher than the king.

draw—A hand that needs additional cards to be of value. "I was on a flush draw," or "I was drawing to a straight." Also: A form of poker.

drawing dead—When there are no cards in the deck that will give you the best hand.

Draw poker—Each player gets five cards, all face-down, and can replace some of his cards with new ones.

duck—A deuce.

early position—Having to act in the first third of players in a hand.

face-down—Cards that are unexposed and thus hidden. A player's hole cards are face-down.

face-up—Exposed, so all players can see what the card is.

fast—An aggressive style of play with a lot of betting and raising. "He played that hand fast."

favorite—Player who has the best chance mathematically to win a hand.

fish—A poor or novice player expected to be easy money.

floorperson—Supervisory cardroom employee who also settles disputes.

flop—The first three community cards exposed in Texas Hold'em. They are turned face-up at the same time. Also, as a verb, to make a hand using just the flop: "I flopped a full house."

fold—To drop out of (quit) a hand. Done by turning one's cards face-down or saying "I fold," "I drop," or "I'm out."

four-flush—Four cards to a flush, with one more needed to complete the hand.

free card—When all players check during a betting round, the next card is considered "free," because no one had to put money in the pot.

freeroll—Tournament in which certain qualifying players get in for free.

garfunkel—A trash offsuit hand such as 8–2, 9–3, 10–4.

goose—Unskilled player.

gutshot—An inside straight draw; also known as a "belly-buster."

heads-up—Game where only two players remain.

hole—A player's unseen (face-down) cards. "I had an ace in the hole."

HORSE—Table that plays five poker games in rotation: Hold'em, Omaha Eight or Better, Razz, Seven-Card Stud, and Seven-Card Stud High-Low Split (Eight or better).

ignorant end—The low end of a straight. If the flop is Q-J-10, and a player has 9-8 in the hole, she has the ignorant end of the straight.

implied odds—What a player feels his actual payoff will be if he hits his hand relative to how much it will cost to play.

in front of—Someone who acts before you in a betting round. "Two players called in front of me."

inside straight draw—A straight draw with only one card that will complete the straight, such as 4-5-6-8.

isolation—Betting, raising, or reraising to try to get heads-up with a weaker hand or weaker player.

joker—Traditionally, a wild card; in modern parlance, a perfect card to complete a hand. "I hit the joker and won a huge pot."

kicker—An unmatched card in a player's hand not used except in ties.

kill—Variation of limit poker; if a player wins two pots in a row, the limits are doubled for the next hand. In a half-kill, the limits are raised 50 percent.

late position—The final third of players to act in a game.

laydown—To fold. "I saved some chips by making a good laydown."

limit—The most that may be bet or raised at any one time.

limit poker—Poker played with limits on the amount that may be bet, as opposed to no-limit, where any amount may be wagered.

limp—To enter a pot by just calling rather than betting or raising. "I limped in to the pot," or "I raised all the limpers."

live blind—A blind that has the option to raise, even if no one has raised the initial blind "bet."

live card—A card whose rank has not appeared on the board or in another hand. "I'm all-in, but at least my hole cards are live."

live one—Player likely to bet wildly and lose a lot of money.

lock—A hand that cannot be beaten.

lock it up—What you tell the floorperson when you want the seat he's holding for you. You have now promised to take that seat.

longshot—A poker hand that has little chance of being made, such as drawing to a hand with four outs or fewer. Also: Any event not expected to occur, such as a horse winning at 50-to-1 odds.

look up—To call someone. "I looked her up and she was bluffing."

loose—A style of play that entails playing a lot of hands, and often playing them too long.

lowball—Style of poker where the worst hand wins.

maniac—A wild, loose player who bets big with questionable cards to build pots.

man with the axe—The king of diamonds.

middle position—The middle third of players to act in a game.

monster—A very, very good hand.

muck—To throw away your hand in a game (fold). "I mucked my hand."

muck pile—The haphazard collection of discards, burn cards, and unused cards in the center of the table.

multiway pot—A hand with more than two players involved.

No-limit—Poker game in which the size of a player's bet is limited only by the amount of money he has on the table.

nuts—The best possible hand given the cards in a particular game.

odds—Chance that a specific event will occur; expressed as a ratio (such as "3-to-1").

offsuit—Two or more cards of different suits.

on the button—The dealer and last to act on every round.

open—To be the first to enter the pot with a raise (in pre-flop action).

open-ended—A straight draw with "both ends open," like 4-5-6-7.

outs—The number of cards left in the deck that will give you the hand you are seeking.

overcall—To call a player's bet after someone else has already called the bet.

overcard—A higher card. If a player has Q-J and the flop is 10-8-6, she has two overcards. If she has Q-J and the flop is A-9-8, one overcard hit the flop.

overlay—Getting better than the correct odds on a bet.

overpair—A higher pair than you can make. If you have Q-J and someone has kings, he has an overpair. If you have jacks and he has kings, he has an overpair.

over the top—To reraise an opponent, especially in no-limit. "He came over the top for all his chips."

overs—When there are some players in a casino game who wish to play a higher limit, they sometimes can play overs; that is, if these players are alone in a hand, the higher limits take effect.

paint—A face card—jacks, queens, and kings.

pat hand—In Draw poker, a hand so good the player doesn't have to draw cards.

pocket—Your two hole (unseen) cards in Hold'em.

pocket pair—Two cards of the same rank in the hole in Hold'em, such as two jacks or two kings.

pocket rockets—Two aces in the hole.

position—Where a player sits relative to the button. The player to the left of the button acts first, and play proceeds clockwise.

positional advantage—When a player acts after another player in a hand.

position bet—When a player bets (or raises) solely on the basis of positional advantage.

post—To put an ante or a blind into the pot. "Please post your blind." Also: In some casinos, to put money up when you first sit down in a game, as an additional blind. "Do I have to post here?"

pot—The chips and money—the sum of all blinds, bets, calls, and raises—put in the center of the table that players compete to win.

pot-limit—Poker game in which a player may bet up to the size of the pot at the time he is making the bet.

pot odds—The size of the pot relative to the cost of calling the bets needed to stay in the hand.

preflop—Before the flop.

protect—When a player has the best hand and bets or raises to get others to fold. "He had to protect his pocket queens."

psychological player—Poker player who relies mostly on "feel" and people skills—reading opponents and predicting what cards they hold—to win.

putting on hands—Figuring out what hand a player is holding by using clues such as body language, betting tactics, and playing style to assign them to a hand.

quads—Four of a kind.

rabbit hunting—Searching through the deck to discover "what might have happened" had a player stayed in a hand.

rag—A low card that apparently helps nobody; also known as a blank.

ragged flop—Low, mismatched cards that seemingly could help no one.

railbird—Person who is standing behind a game, just watching; often a player who has busted out of the game.

rainbow—Cards of all different suits. "It was a rainbow flop."

raise—Increasing the amount players must pay to stay in a hand, done by adding chips to another player's original bet.

rake—Money taken out of every pot by the House. The House's take.

ram—To bet and raise powerfully and often during a hand. Also know as "ram and jam."

Razz—Seven-Card Stud where the worst hand wins. 5-4-3-2-A is the perfect low.

read—To figure out a player by studying his personality, mannerisms, expressions, and style of play. "I had a good read on him."

rebuy—Buying more chips in a poker tournament when a player's stack falls below a certain level.

represent—When a player bets and acts as if she has a particular hand. "She was representing a straight."

reraise—To raise someone who has previously raised.

re-reraise—To raise someone who has reraised. Thus if there was a bet, a raise, a reraise, and a re-reraise, it would cost a player four bets to stay in the hand.

ring game—A standard nontournament game.

river—The fifth and final community card in Hold'em and Omaha. It is dealt separately. Also: The last card dealt in any game.

rivered—To make a hand on the river, as in "I rivered a queen to win the pot."

rock—A tight, conservative player who plays only premium hands and takes few risks.

rolled up—Three of a kind in the first three cards in Seven-Card Stud.

runner-runner—Catching two perfect cards on the end to win. "I got runner-runner spades for the flush!"

running—Two consecutive cards, usually the last two cards dealt in a game. "I caught two running hearts for the flush!"

rush—Winning a higher-than-expected number of hands in a short time. Also known as a "hot streak."

safety zone—Area where a player feels comfortable and at ease with the stakes and limits. Comfort zone.

sandbagging—Slow-playing a hand to induce an opponent to bet. Also know as check-raise.

satellite—A minitournament, usually one table, in which the prize is an entry fee into the main tournament.

scare card—A card that seems to greatly benefit a player. "A scare card hit the turn."

scoop—To win the entire pot in a split-pot game.

4—Fee collected from each player on the hour or half-hour in high-stakes casino poker games in lieu of a rake.

see—To call someone's bet. "I'll see your ten dollars," or "I'll see that bet." Generally not used in today's poker slang.

set—Three of a kind in Hold'em consisting of a pair in a player's hand and a matching card on the board.

sheriff—Someone who calls other players to make sure they aren't bluffing.

short-handed—A game with four or fewer players.

short pair—A pair below jacks in Draw (Jacks or Better) poker.

short-stacked—To have the fewest chips at the table, especially in a tournament.

showdown—When, after all betting in a hand is completed, the players expose their hands and determine a winner.

side game—A standard ring (nontournament) game. "I busted out of the tournament early, but I found a very profitable side game."

side pot—After a player has gone all-in, others in the hand may continue to bet and raise, but their money is placed in a separate pot. The all-in player is not eligible to win the side pot.

slow—A style of play with lots of checking and calling and not much betting and raising.

slow-play—Playing a top hand in a weak manner to disguise its strength. "He trapped me by slow-playing those three aces."

small blind—Located to the left of the button, the smaller of the two forced "blind bets" in community-card games. It's generally half the size of the big blind and placed in the pot before cards are dealt.

smooth call—To call a bet with a very strong hand, rather than raising.

spit—A community card placed face-up in the center of the table. Often used in stud games when there are not sufficient cards left in the deck to complete all players' hands.

split pair—In a stud game, having a pair with one card in the hole, the other on the board.

stack—How many chips a player has.

stakes—The amount of money being played for; also, the limits of the game.

standing pat—Playing your original five cards in Draw poker; that is, not drawing any cards.

starting hand—Cards dealt to a player before the first bet.

stealing—Bluffing. "I'm not going to let you steal the pot."

steaming—Same as *tilt*.

stone-cold bluff—A bluff with a hand so weak that it has no chance of winning unless all other players fold.

straddle—When the player to the left of the big blind puts in a raise before being dealt a hand. With a "live" straddle, he is last to act in the first round and may raise his own bet.

street—A betting round. "She bet on fourth street" means she bet after the fourth card.

string bet—Illegal move where a player puts chips in the pot and then returns to his stack for more, rather than betting in a continuous motion.

Stud poker—Some of a player's cards are face-down, others face-up. There are no community cards.

suck-out—To outdraw someone on the river. "That guy is a real suck-out artist."

suicide king—The king of hearts.

suited—Two or more cards of the same suit.

suited connectors—Two or more cards of the same suit in sequence. For instance, in Hold'em, hole cards that are the 10♥ and 9♥.

super satellite—A multitable tournament in which the prizes are one or more entries into a major event.

swing—The fluctuation sustained by a player's chip count during a given session. "It was a wild game. I had a huge swing today."

table image—Someone's personality and playing style as perceived by other players.

table stakes—Stakes wherein a player is limited to betting or calling with the chips and cash she has on the table. She cannot be bet out of a pot because she does not have enough capital.

taking a card off—Just calling with the intention of seeing another card as cheaply as possible and likely folding if the hand does not improve.

technical player—A poker player who relies mostly on mathematical calculations to make decisions.

tell—A mannerism, expression, action, or other unintentional clue that reveals a player's hand, personality, or strategy.

tight—Conservative, cautious strategy; playing very few hands.

tilt—When someone begins playing wildly due to emotional upset; also known as *steaming*. "He suffered two bad beats and went on *tilt*."

toke—Poker players' term for a tip.

top kicker—Best possible kicker in a community-card game. If the Hold'em board is 8-7-2 and a player has A-8 in the pocket, he has the top pair with the top kicker.

top pair—In a community-card game, when a player has paired a hole card with the highest card on the board.

trap—To underplay a hand until other players bet, and then punish them with raises.

trips—Common term for three of a kind.

turn—The fourth community card in Hold'em and Omaha, dealt separately.

underdog—Player not favored to win a hand; also called a *dog*.

underpair—A pair that is "under" the board in a community-card game. If the board is 9-8-7 and a player has pocket fives, he has an underpair.

under the gun—The player to the left of the big blind, who must act first during the initial betting round.

unsuited—Two or more cards of different suits.

up-card—One of a player's face-up (exposed) cards in a stud game.

value bet—When a player bets a hand that is not a sure thing but feels that the bet, over time, will win more than it loses.

wheel—A five-high straight, that is, 5-4-3-2-A. Also called a "bicycle."

wired—To have a pair in the hole from the start. "I had aces wired."

WPT—The World Poker Tour. A series of high buy-in Hold'em tournaments televised on the Travel channel, culminating with a $25,000 buy-in event at the Bellagio resort/casino in Vegas.

wrap—In Omaha, four cards in sequence in the hole, such as 7-8-9-10.

WSOP—The World Series of Poker. A string of big-money tournaments held at the Rio casino in Las Vegas each spring.

Appendix C
Book'em!
Further Reading

24/7, by Andres Martinez, Villard Books/Random House, New York, 1999.

Against the Gods: The Remarkable Story of Risk, by Peter L. Bernstein, John Wiley & Sons, New York, 1998.

The Arm, by Clark Howard, Sherbourne Press Inc., Los Angeles, 1967.

Beneath the Neon, by Michael "London" Haywood, Carlton Press, New York, 1984.

Big Deal, by Anthony Holden, Viking/Penguin, New York, 1990.

The Biggest Game in Town, by A. Alvarez, Houghton Mifflin, Boston, 1983.

The Complete Book of Hold'em Poker, by Gary Carson, Lyle Stuart/Kensington Publishing Group, New York, 2001.

The Everything® Poker Strategy Book, by John Wenzel, Adams Media, Avon, MA, 2004.

Gambling Secrets of Nick the Greek, by Ted Thackrey Jr., Rand McNally & Co., Chicago, 1968.

Getting the Best of It, by David Sklansky, self-published, 1982, 1989.

How to Figure the Odds on Everything, by Darrell Huff, Dreyfus Publications Ltd., New York, 1972.

Inside Las Vegas, by Mario Puzo, Grosset & Dunlap, New York, 1977.

Johnny Moss: Champion of Champions, by Don Jenkins, JM Publishing, 1981.

King of a Small World, by Rick Bennet, Arcade Publishing, New York, 1995.

Loaded Dice, by John Soares, Taylor Publishing Co., Dallas, TX, 1985.

Mike Caro's the Book of Tells, by Mike Caro, Gambling Times Inc., Hollywood, CA, 1984.

Nick the Greek, King of the Gamblers, by Cy Rice, Funk & Wagnalls, New York, 1969.

No Fold'em Hold'em, by D. R. Sherer, Poker Plus Publications, Las Vegas, 1997.

Play Poker Like the Pros, by Phil Hellmuth Jr., HarperCollins Publishers, Inc., New York, 2003.

Poker! (Las Vegas Style), by Bill "Bulldog" Sykes, Bulldog Publishing, Las Vegas, 1992.

Poker: The Real Deal, by Phil Gordon and Jonathan Grotenstein, Simon & Schuster, Inc., New York, 2004.

Shuffle Up and Deal, by Mike Sexton, HarperCollins Publishers, Inc., New York, 2005.

Shut Up and Deal, by Jesse May, Anchor Books Doubleday, New York, 1998.

Small Stakes Hold'em, by Ed Miller, David Sklansky, and Mason Malmuth, Two Plus Two Publishing, Las Vegas, 2004.

Super System 2, by Doyle Brunson, Cardoza Publishing, New York, 2005.

Tap City, by Ron Abell, Little Brown & Co., Boston, 1985.

Texas Bill's Winning a Living, by William T. Melms, self-published, 1998.

Total Poker, by David Spanier, Simon & Schuster, New York, 1977.

Tournament Poker and the Art of War, by David Apostolico, Lyle Stuart Books, New York, 2005.

Winner's Guide to Texas Hold'em Poker, by Ken Warren, Cardoza Publishing, New York, 1996.

Zen and the Art of Poker, by Larry W. Phillips, Penguin Putnam, Inc., New York, 1999.

Index